WHAT CUMBERLAND PRESBYTERIANS BELIEVE

(REVISED)

Ewell K. Reagin

WHAT CUMBERLAND PRESBYTERIANS BELIEVE

EWELL K. REAGIN

2014

Historical Foundation
of the Cumberland Presbyterian Church
and the Cumberland Presbyterian Church in America

Memphis, Tennessee

What Cumberland Presbyterians Believe. Digital formatting and design by Matthew H. Gore for the Historical Foundation of the Cumberland Presbyterian Church and the Cumberland Prebyterian Church in America. Entire contents ©2011 by the Historical Foundation.

Originally published in 1931.

September 2014.

Historical Foundation
Cumberland Presbyterian Church &
Cumberland Presbyterian Church in America
8207 Traditional Place
Cordova (Memphis), Tennessee 38016

ISBN: 978-0-6156-9966-0

Introduction: 2011

If there is any book (aside from the Holy Bible and the Cumberland Presbyterian Confession of Faith, of course) that belongs in every Cumberland Presbyterian home, every Cumberland Presbyterian church library, and in the hands of every Cumberland Presbyterian minister and elder, it is this one. The number of persons who experienced Ewell K. Reagin's preaching and teaching grows smaller every year, but his influence continues through his writing ministry. The Pastoral Development Ministry Team (and before them, the Commission on Ministry) gives a copy of this book to every new candidate for ministry. Students at Memphis Theological Seminary and the Program of Alternate Studies search for guidance in these pages. Pastors, elders, Sunday school teachers, and church members read these words to better understand the doctrines of our denomination. Yes, the influence of this book will endure for quite some time.

Whether you are outside our fellowship and wondering what we these people called Cumberland Presbyterians believe, already a Cumberland Presbyterian and wondering just what that means, or looking for a resource to teach the doctrines of the Cumberland Presbyterian Church, you have come to the right place. This book is a perfect resource for family or individual study. Taken chapter by chapter, it also makes outstanding curriculum for a Sunday school class, membership class, youth group, or other small group.

Reagin's writing style is accessible and understandable, but an unfortunate difficulty in reading this work today is that all allusions to the Confession of Faith refer to the 1883 version. Since Reagin died in 1985, he did not re-edit to accommodate the structural and language changes made in the 1984 revision of the Confession. But fear not, for this problem is easily overcome. Before reading each chapter of this book, simply read the corresponding sections of the 1984 Confession of Faith and their associated scripture references.

> For Chapter 2, read sections 5.01 through 5.09 in the 1984 Confession.
> For Chapter 3, read sections 1.04 through 1.07.
> For Chapter 4, read sections 1.01 through 1.03 and 1.13 through 1.18.
> For Chapter 5, read sections 3.07 through 3.11 and 4.01 through 4.04.

For Chapter 6, read 4.12 through 4.23 and 6.06 through 6.09.
For Chapter 7, read 4.24 through 4.26.
For Chapters 8 and 9, read 5.18 through 5.22.
For Chapter 10, read 5.23 through 5.27.
For Chapter 11, read sections 7.01 through 7.08.

You will likely find in these pages some things which you take for granted and some things which challenge your thinking. Reagin reportedly claimed to be neither a liberal nor a fundamentalist. He further claimed that he strove to be "sensible and generous" with those who held views and opinions different from his. Such attitudes and actions may very well be what made him such a good Cumberland Presbyterian. May your time in this indispensable work make you a good Cumberland Presbyterian as well.

Andy McClung, *D.Min.*

Editor's Note

Observant readers and *book people* will notice that the usual publishing conventions for the use of Roman numerals and Arabic numerals to paginate different portions of a volume are not strictly followed. While we don't believe this to be a major issue, a word of explanation does seem to be in order. In general practice, the first page of the main body of a book is numbered "1" and all preceding pages are numbered with Roman numerals beginning with the first flyleaf. Prior printings of this book did not follow this practice and started with Arabic numerals on the very first page of the book. In order that groups might use this edition with any other printing of the 1968 revision and have all readers on the same page, so to speak, we have retained the page numbering of those previous printings. So, page 7 in this printing has the same text as page 7 in the 2006 printing. Thank you for your understanding.

Matthew H. Gore

Ewell K. Reagin

1

Preface to the Sixth Edition

This book was prepared and published at the request of the Board of Publication and Christian Education in 1931, and it has been revised or reprinted at their request in 1939, 1946, 1961, 1968 and now in 1979. The ideas were first presented as sermons in the First Cumberland Presbyterian Church in Knoxville, Tennessee, and were then prepared for publication under the title, *The Essence of Our Faith.* After the author had taught a course related to the subject in various camps and conferences over the church, he made changes which would make it more suitable to that purpose, and the Board began to publish it under the present title.

The author claims no originality for any of this work. Many sources have been used freely in the effort to present to those who are interested a simple interpretation of the chief doctrines upon which the faith of our denomination is based.

There have been several changes in the text during the various revisions, and one major change was made in this present edition. Chapter 2, "The Church," was rewritten to give a more complete description of what we consider to be the nature and mission of the church. All other parts of the book remain as they were in the 1961 edition.

The author strongly suggests that you consult as a companion volume to this work his more complete study of the Confession of Faith entitled *We Believe and So We Speak;* his most recent works, *Truth Stones of the Bible,* will be a help in the study of chapters 3 and 11, and *The Holy Spirit,* a help in connection with Chapter 5.

Knoxville, Tennessee

E. K. Reagin

August 21, 1979

WHAT CUMBERLAND PRESBYTERIAN BELIEVE

5

_1_

Our Family
Background

The Cumberland Presbyterian Church gets its name from two sources. The first of these sources is purely geographic. It happened that when this branch of the Presbyterian Church originated, it started in a section of Tennessee and Kentucky which was called the Cumberland Country. Because of this designation, the people who joined this group came to be known as Cumberland Presbyterians. It was a simple way of setting apart a particular group of Presbyterians, who shared a form of government with those in other "Presbyterian" churches.

The second part of our name comes from the type of doctrine and government which we accept. Although the Cumberland Presbyterian Church has modified the government and doctrines of the Presbyterian faith, it is still generally Presbyterian in its character. For that reason the church is called the Cumberland Presbyterian Church. But we need to notice more carefully just what is meant by the Presbyterian part of the name.

What Does Presbyterian Mean?

The name Presbyterian comes from the Bible. Of course, the name does not occur in the English Bible, but the Bible was not written originally in English. The Old Testament was written in Hebrew, and the New Testament in Greek. From these original languages various translations have been made until we have the Bible in our own language. It is from the Greek that we get the word from which we derive the name Presbyterian. This word occurs about sixty times in the Greek New Testament and about one hundred times in the Greek translation of the Old Testament. By substituting English letters for the Greek letters in this word we get the word "presbyter." From this word "presbyter" we get our name "Presbyterian" because we are governed by presbyters. The English meaning of this Greek word is our word elder. A presbyter is an elder, and an elder is a presbyter. We are all quite familiar with the word elder and have seen it in the Bible many times.

A certain teacher in a Baptist seminary recently made the statement, "The Presbyterian church has the nearest thing to what some of us find in the Bible as an organized government."

Is Presbyterianism in the Bible?

The Presbyterian church really began back in Bible times. In Acts 14:23 we are told that Paul and Barnabas ordained elders in the churches which they organized. In Acts 20:17 we learn that Paul sent for the elders of the church at Ephesus to meet him at Miletus. In Titus 1:5 Paul commands Titus to ordain elders in every city. These are a few of the New Testament passages which show that the New Testament church was ruled by elders.

The Old Testament church was also ruled by elders. In Exodus 3:16 the Lord commands Moses to call the elders of Israel together. In Numbers 11:16 the Lord tells Moses to gather seventy of the elders of Israel whom he knew to be elders and officers over the people. There are many other passages in the Old Testament which show that the church of that time was ruled by elders.

No one would claim that the elders of the Old Testament worshiping community had exactly the same duties as elders in our churches today, but the same principle of representative government is there.

Presbyterians are sometimes troubled when they find the word "bishop" in the Bible. The term occurs five times and is sometimes interpreted to indicate that our system of government is not really the Biblical system. But if a more careful study of the passages is made, it will be seen that the bishops are simply elders.

In Acts 20:17 Paul sends for the elders of the church at Ephesus, and in Acts 20:28 he calls them bishops, or overseers. In Titus 1:5 Paul directs that elders should be ordained in every city, and in Titus 1:7 he calls these same men bishops. The bishop of the New Testament was not a bishop in the modern sense of the word, but was an elder. New Testament elders never dreamed of the authority which is accorded modern bishops. Theirs was a work of perfect equality.

"Let the elders that rule well be counted worthy of double honor, especially they who labor in the word and doctrine" (I Timothy 5:17). This passage clearly teaches that some elders had the additional duty of labor in word and doctrine. Upon this basis the Presbyterian churches have developed their system of ruling elders and preaching elders. Every church has a pastor, or preaching elder, and a group of ruling elders. The pastor and the ruling elders constitute the session, which is the governing body of the Cumberland Presbyterian Church.

There is strong evidence that the elders in the New Testament church were elected by the people. In Acts 1:15-26 all the disciples at Jerusalem took part in the election of a man to fill the place of Judas. In Acts 6:3 all the disciples took part in the election of the seven deacons. In Acts 14:23 we are told that they ordained elders in every church. There is good evidence in this passage that the people elected the elders by the showing of hands, since the passage is literally translated "chosen by the show of hands."

In the early church the election of church officers by the vote of the people is a conspicuous part of the church government. Clement of Rome, writing about 100 A. D., says that church officers received their offices "by consent of the whole church."

These passages, with the many others that might be produced, seem sufficient to show that, during the many years of the Christian church, the body has been ruled by representatives who are called elders and that they were elected by the people over whom they ruled. It is just this system, which has been preserved by all Presbyterian bodies throughout the years, which is the form of government used by the Cumberland Presbyterian Church.

What Is the Place of Deacons?

Deacons have no more part in the government of the Cumberland Presbyterian Church than other members of the congregation, but they are officers of the church who are set apart for a particular purpose.

Deacons are mentioned in only two passages in the New Testament (Philippians 1:1 and 1 Timothy 3:10-13). They are mentioned in Philippians and their qualifications are given in Timothy. Nowhere are their duties defined. If the "seven" who were chosen, as described in the sixth chapter of Acts, were deacons, as is generally supposed, their duties are very clearly given.

"The seven" were chosen in order that they might take the burden of caring for the poor from the shoulders of the apostles, in order that the apostles might give more time to their preaching and to prayer. Their business was to attend to the material work of the church. From this we have concluded that deacons should attend to the temporal and financial affairs of the church, and thus leave the elders and the pastor free to spend their time in doing the things which are connected with the more spiritual matters.

Does the Bible Justify Presbyteries?

We have seen that individual congregations are governed by the preaching and ruling elders, who constitute the session. We have also seen that this system was in practice in Biblical days. Now the question remains: Were these Biblical churches bound together by some principal, such as ours, which makes our congregation into presbyteries, synods, and the General Assembly? We feel that this question can be answered in the affirmative, and that our system of representative group bound together for the sake of mutual helpfulness has the endorsement of scripture.

When the great question about church membership arose in the congregation at Antioch, why did they not just get together and decide what they would do? If they had been a congregation entirely separate from all others, they probably would have done that. But instead of that procedure they referred the matter to a council of church people at Jerusalem. This council is described in Acts the fifteenth chapter. It was composed of apostles and elders who, after full deliberation, settled the question with authority and sent their decision back to the church at Antioch. And not only did the church at Antioch accept the decision; it became a working principle for all churches. There was a tie which bound them together in a way similar to the way in which our churches are bound together in presbyteries, synods, and the General Assembly.

An interesting passage in this connection is I Timothy 4:14, when Paul exhorts Timothy not to neglect the gift which came to him "with the laying on of the hands of the presbytery." Here in the Bible we find the very word and the very system which can be seen at any presbytery of the Cumberland Presbyterian Church where anyone is set apart to the full work of the ministry.

Is Presbyterianism Reflected In Our Government?

This system resembles our general national system of government. The churches of a certain district are organized into a presbytery which is similar to our county government. Several of these presbyteries are combined into a synod which, generally speaking, resembles our state government. Then, in turn, these synods and presbyteries combine to form our General Assembly, which is similar to our national government. Or, to make the case a little clearer, these church courts can be compared to our civil courts. The presbytery is like the county court. The synod is a court of appeal to supervise or settle cases that are brought to it from the local courts. And the General Assembly is the supreme court which settles finally upon all matters, the national Congress which gives laws for the direction of the whole body.

How Has Presbyterianism Developed?

It is a long step from Biblical times to the organization of the Cumberland Presbyterian Church in America. But, because of limitations set by the purpose of this discussion, we shall cover only briefly the beginnings of the Presbyterian Church in America and the events of its history which preceded the organization of our church. From general church history one can trace the program of the church through the eighteen hundred years before the organization of our denomination as it developed into a large body of people with varying interests and tastes; as corrupt practices came in, which occasioned the Protestant Reformation, in which all Protestant denominations had their beginning; and, finally, as these denominations began to grow in the New World.

The Presbyterians who settled in America came from many different parts of Europe and from several nationalities. Some of them came from England and settled in Salem, Charleston, and Boston; some came from Holland and settled in New York; some were from France and settled in Virginia, South Carolina, New York and other places. The Scotch Presbyterians settled in New York, South Carolina, New Jersey and other places. Many German Presbyterians settled in Pennsylvania and made their way south into Virginia and North Carolina. These people were strangers to one another in a strange and unsettled country. The record of how they were able to work together and to develop a great church is inspiring.

According to tradition, the father of American Presbyterianism was a young man who came from Ireland at the age of twenty-five. This young man, Francis Makemie, was ordained by the Presbytery of Laggan in North Ireland in 1683 and came at once to America. He was an unusual worker, with a genius for leadership and organization. Within a year after his arrival, he had organized several Presbyterian churches near his home on the eastern shore of Maryland. In 1705 or 1706, in or near Philadelphia, Makemie organized the first American presbytery. The exact time and place are not certain, because the first page of the old minutes of that meeting has been lost. This presbytery was called the Presbytery of Philadelphia; and, although there were only seven ministers and "certain elders" present, it was a great beginning. From this start, organized Presbyterianism in our country is dated.

About the time of this organization, the great tide of Scotch-Irish emigrants set in, and Presbyterianism began to grow more rapidly. From 1705 to 1775, one historian estimates that 500,000 Scotch-Irish came to this country and became the backbone of Presbyterianism. Perhaps it was the influence of this rapid growth which enabled the church to grow from one presbytery in 1705 to four presbyteries in 1717.

With this rapid growth, organization began to be developed; and in 1717 the first synod was organized at Philadelphia. There were seventeen ministers and a few elders present at this meeting. Although the Presbyterian Church in America at that time had only nineteen ministers, forty churches, and three thousand members, the foundation for a great movement was being laid.

What Divisions Has Presbyterianism Suffered?

The first of the many divisions of the Presbyterian Church in America, caused largely by the attitude of different groups toward evangelistic methods, came in 1741. About 1735, a great religious revival began under the leadership of the Reverend Gilbert Tennent, who was the son of the Reverend William Tennent, the founder of "The Log College," which sent a great many young men into the ministry. Young Gilbert Tennent did not conform to the old customs. Among other things, he refused to wear a powdered wig and the regular ministerial dress, and preferred to wear a coat girded about with a leather girdle. Also, this young evangelist preached a sermon on "The Unconverted Ministry," which he intended for the preachers who opposed the revival. Because of this breach between the revival party and the anti-revival party, the church divided into the New Side, or the revival party, and the Old Side, or anti-revival party.

Another point about which the New Side and the Old Side disagreed was the question of education. The Old Side wanted the ministers trained in the universities of Scotland. The New Side wanted to train their ministers in such schools as the Log College, in America. There were no doctrinal differences between the New Side and the Old Side; but, as in the case of the organization of the Cumberland Presbyterian Church, they disagreed on methods and practices.

During the time of the division between the New Side and the Old Side, the church made rapid progress. The New Side ministers deserve the greater credit for this progress, because they were generally young men and were more evangelistic than the Old Side ministers. One of these ministers was Samuel Davies, a young man twenty-four years of age, who came to Hanover County, Virginia, in 1747. In 1775 he organized Hanover Presbytery, which included everything south of the Potomac and was the beginning of organized Presbyterianism in the South. He left Virginia in 1759 to become president of Princeton College. Another New Side minister was Alexander Craighead, who was quite prominent in the revival in the section around Charlotte, North Carolina. Hugh McAden is an interesting preacher of the New Side group. He did much preaching in the Valley of Virginia, North Carolina and South Carolina; and his diary is one of the most interesting books in Presbyterian history.

In 1758 the Old Side and the New Side were again united into one church, as the Synod of New York and Philadelphia. At this time there were ninety-eight ministers, two hundred churches and ten thousand members. For the next several years the church went forward in its work, organized many Christian schools, did missionary work among the Indians, and tried to meet the needs of the growing population. By 1775 there were one hundred forty ministers, three hundred churches and eighteen thousand members.

The American Revolution was not only a struggle for civil liberty, but it was also a struggle for religious liberty. The Episcopal Church was the established church in nearly all of the colonies, and members of all the other denominations were taxed to support that church. In some of the colonies, ministers and members of denominations other than the Episcopal Church were persecuted for preaching their particular doctrines and carrying on their practices. The revolution was partly an uprising against this religious oppression. Historians tell us that "the first voice publicly lifted in America to dissolve all connection with Great Britain came not from the Puritans of New England, nor the Dutch of New York, nor the planters of Virginia, but from the Scotch-Irish Presbyterians." They also take note of the fact that the Presbyterians had a large share in the movements which led up to the Declaration of Independence and a large part in the actual Revolutionary War which followed. They also had a great part in shaping the Constitution of the United States.

What Was the Immediate Background of Our Church?

It was while the statesmen were busy writing the Constitution that Presbyterian leaders were busy organizing a nation-wide Presbyterian Church. In 1789 the General Assembly was organized in Philadelphia. In that same year George Washington became President of the United States, and very cordial letters were passed between the new Assembly and the President. With the organization of this national body the church was now prepared to go forward more efficiently than ever.

French infidelity had a great influence upon America in the latter part of the eighteenth century. Histories of the times indicate that spirituality was at a very low ebb during those days. Moreover, the population was increasing rapidly, and people were settling new and large territories. The church had a great task before it.

At about this time, another great revival of religion swept over the country, and with it some excesses in revival practices. To some of the church leaders, these revival methods were objectionable, while others approved them, just as in the days of the New Side and the Old Side division. Also, the revival brought many new people into the church and thus created need for more leaders to teach them.

It was from this background that the Cumberland Presbyterian Church had its start. The Cumberland Presbyterian ministers were members of the revival party. They were also in favor of meeting the emergency created by the enlarged church by ordaining ministers to look after the new converts and churches, even if they did not meet with the educational standards set by the Presbyterian Church. It was not that they were opposed to education, but that they wanted to meet an emergency. They did not agree with all of the teachings of the *Westminster Confession,* but they had the clear right to disagree.

The manner in which the denomination was started on February 4, 1810, is known to practically all Cumberland Presbyterians and will not be repeated here. It is still a denomination with a rich background, a sound system of doctrines, and a compelling mission.

2

Characteristics
of Our Church

From the standpoint of organization, there are three main types of churches. On one extreme is the Episcopal type which has a bishop, or some other such ruler, at its head from whom all orders come and whose word is the final authority. This type of church is represented in America by such denominations as the Roman Catholic, the Episcopal, and the Methodist. There are variations in all of these bodies, but the type of organization is essentially the same.

The second type of government is the Representative type, which is characterized by the rule of men or women who have been elected by the group. They band themselves together in various types of regional groups and agree to abide by the decisions of their chosen representatives. This type is represented in America chiefly by the Presbyterian and Reformed bodies.

On the other extreme is the Congregational type. The character of this type is that each local congregation makes its own laws, decides on its own doctrines and practices, and thinks of itself as a separate unit, largely independent of all other units. The denominations with which we are most familiar in this group are the various types of Baptists, the Disciples (Christian churches), and the Churches of God.

The manner of ordaining ministers and passing laws reveals rather clearly the characters of the various groups. In the Episcopal type, the minister is always under the direction of superior officers. The bishop ordains the minister and the laws or orders are passed from the head office down to the next in authority and finally on down to the people. In the Presbyterian, or representative type, the minister is ordained by the presbytery which is composed of ministers and elected representatives from the local churches. These elected representatives also vote on the orders and laws and agree among themselves what they will do. In the Congregational type each congregation ordains its own ministers and agrees on whatever procedures or doctrines it chooses and is not finally responsible to any larger group.

It will be seen from this brief discussion that from the stand point of church government, our church, along with other Presbyterian bodies, is not extreme one way or the other. The congregations exist as units and have a voice in the affairs of the church as a whole, but they also have some authority over one another and are submissive to the authority of others for their mutual good. This form of government, as was stated in chapter 1, is very much like the form of political government under which we live in America.

While we are Presbyterian in theory and practice, it should be noted that there are differences in the way Presbyterians carry on their organization. The three bodies of Presbyterians with which we are most familiar are the United Presbyterian Church in the U.S.A., the Presbyterian Church, U.S., and the Cumberland Presbyterian. While all of these are representative in government, the United Presbyterian Church tends to place more authority in the General Assembly and boards of the church. Their moderator seems to have greater authority and voice than the moderator of any of the other branches. In the Presbyterian Church, U.S. (sometimes called Southern Presbyterian) the presbytery seems to exercise more authority than in the United Presbyterian Church. In the Cumberland Presbyterian Church, while we have the same offices, we have a tendency, whether it be considered good or bad, to give more authority to the congregation. These are not theoretical variations, but developmental, having come about in our separateness during the years.

From the standpoint of doctrine, there are, generally speaking, two main classes of belief. The Calvinistic group believes that man's salvation depends upon the choice of God who is solely responsible for the salvation of every individual. At the other extreme are the Arminian groups who believe that man has a determining part in deciding his own salvation. Every individual, according to this doctrine, will be saved or lost because of what he does or his ability to remain true to the end of his life.

In between these extremes there is a medium theology which is neither strictly Calvinistic nor strictly Arminian. This medium theology is accepted by Cumberland Presbyterians, both in theory and in practice. Our church is not alone in this position because many people, regardless of their church name, believe a similar doctrine. According to this belief, the responsibility for our salvation is *upon God and man.* But there is a balance of these two forces which makes salvation neither an arbitrary matter on the part of God nor a question of man's works alone. *(This subject is further discussed in chapters 6 and 7.*

Our Church Among the Churches

The Cumberland Presbyterian Church considers itself a part of the universal Church of Jesus Christ. Section 99 of our Confession of Faith says that we believe in the unity of all believers of all time. Since we believe that people in Old Testament times were saved through the work of the Holy Spirit, just as we are, this means that they were also in the church. The church of God did not begin on the day of Pentecost. It had a revival on that day, but it was already in existence. Regardless of the question of time or place, the church is one and Christ is its head.

Also in Section 99, we show that we consider ourselves to be a cooperative church. We have never felt nor taught that ours is the only church. We recognize as members of the church in this world all those who are members of like bodies of Christians. Since we designate that there must be some "formal covenant with God and some organized body of Christians" (Section 1(0), we are opposed to such groups as band themselves together as independents. The church must be a body.

Also in Section 100 of the Confession of Faith, it is stated that "the children of such (meaning those who have entered into a formal covenant) are included in the covenant relations of their parents, and are properly under the special care of the Church." In some denominations such children are considered "members of the church." In our own denomination there are some who speak of them in the same way, but it is evident from our practices that we do not mean to imply that all children of believing parents, or even all baptized children, are "members of the church." What is evidently meant by our statement and our practice is that they are "included in the covenant relations of their parents, and are properly under the special care of the Church." We maintain a roll of baptized children and are instructed to report them annually in our statistical reports. The instructions tell us to report the number of "baptized children of believing parents who have not become full members of the church. These are not to be counted in the total membership."

Since they are included with their parents, when letters are granted to the parents, the names of such baptized children are noted. These instances are cited to indicate what our actual practice is regarding the children in the church. They are "under the special care of the church" but to become "full members" requires an action on their part similar to that for adults.

What Is Distinctive About Our Church?

From the preceding discussion, it is evident that the Cumberland Presbyterian Church differs from other churches in some respects, and it is like others in many other respects. The likenesses far exceed the differences. Like all Protestant bodies, we accept the Bible as our basis of authority in faith and conduct. We believe in Christ as the supreme revelation of God and the divine

Savior of men. We regard Christ as the only head of the church. And in all matters which really affect man's salvation and his Christian life we are in practical agreement. There must be some distinguishing characteristics or we would not continue to exist as a distinct body. Even if they are rather general in some ways, they exist and should be recognized.

We have already seen some of the differences between the branches of the Presbyterian family. In chapter 4 you will discover some of the major differences between us and other Presbyterians in regard to theology.

We are different from the Protestant Episcopal Church in our form of government and type of worship. We are not accustomed, generally speaking, to the use of the Prayer Book and other types of ritualistic worship. This difference also applies to the Lutheran churches.

Our difference with the Methodist Church is one of governmental form and on the question of the preservation of believers from a doctrinal standpoint. We are sometimes referred to facetiously as "Methodist Presbyterians," but we would insist that our leanings toward Arminianism are not strong enough to justify this description.

We differ from Baptists in our form of government and in several doctrinal matters. To us baptism is not a door into the church, nor is it a symbol of the death, burial, and resurrection of Jesus. Our differences with them on the nature of the church is perhaps signified by the different attitudes toward the Lord's Supper. We do not refuse anybody at the Lord's table, but invite any who believe in Christ to partake with us. Individual Baptist churches may differ on this, as well as any other doctrine or practice, but the practice of communion by congregations is a common characteristic of Baptists.

Our differences with the Christian Churches, or Disciples of Christ, are on the matters of government and on the question of the importance of water baptism. We reject the idea that baptism must be by immersion alone and that it is necessary to salvation.

So, the distinctions might be continued with all other branches of the church, including the Roman Catholics and the Greek Orthodox. There are differences which are not mere matters of personal preference, but of real importance. But there are many similarities which are also very important and which enable us to work together as Christians in spite of the ways we have grown apart during the years.

These similarities and differences do not constitute our distinctive characteristics. What makes us and keeps us a separate body of Christians who live under a different banner and with a different name? Perhaps the most distinctive thing about us is that while we have many things in common with all of these other bodies, none of them has all the points of doctrine and government which we claim as our own. The later chapters of this book will show what they are.

Just as in government and theology our church is in the middle position, so usually in social classes it has appealed to what we commonly refer to as the middle class. While our work is not limited to this class, our congregations are usually located in geographic areas where the majority are in this social position. The majority of our congregations are located in rural sections, although the majority of our members are in towns and cities. One of our big problems is that we have so many very small congregations which are not able to do much more than maintain their own existence.

Although our church was in existence at the time of the Civil War, it did not divide over the war or slavery, and is today the same church both in the North and in the South. The majority of our congregations, however, are in the South.

Our congregations seem generally to favor what is called "free worship," which is not restricted by a ritual. There are wide variations in this, however, and we have a few churches which could scarcely be distinguished from the liturgical groups. Since the church started in the days of the "Great Awakening" of 1800, we are generally classed as a "revival church," and properly so. Our doctrine of "whosoever will" makes the presentation of the gospel to all people a matter of great importance.

Because of the wide variations of beliefs and practices in a small denomination scattered over eighteen states of the United States and some foreign countries, it is difficult to give characteristics which cannot be challenged. The reader may think of other distinctive marks of his church which make it distinctly his.

How Do We Become Members of the Church?

Section 99 of our Confession of Faith says that those who "have become children of God by faith" are in the church. Section 100 says that the members of the church are those who "hold to the fundamental doctrines of Christianity" and "have entered into a formal covenant with God and some organized body of Christians." In order to understand among ourselves whether or not the persons who desire to become members of the church conform to these requirements, we require all persons to appear before the elders of the church, whom we call the session, and answer some questions regarding these matters. In our Directory for Worship, five questions are set forth as a "recommended" form of church covenant.

The first question asked prospective members regards their belief about the Bible. This is the only question among the five which has to do with the matter of belief. Notice also that it is a rather broad question since it asks simply that one state whether or not he believes that the Bible is "the only infallible rule of faith and practice." What one believes about the Bible or what one believes about other things is not specifically stated. Our church is satisfied if one accepts the Bible as the standard for what he believes and for the way he lives the Christian life. This question can be compared with our doctrinal statements in Sections 1-6 of the Confession of Faith. Also, questions 1-12 of the Catechism have to do with a similar idea.

The second question of the church covenant relates to our Christian experience. Our church seeks to know what the prospective member has experienced with regard to sin and salvation. The question asks if one has experienced a need for Christ as Savior and the salvation which he offers to give. Since the individual is the only one who can answer this question, the session merely asks if this has been experienced as a fact. If you are interested in comparing this statement with our doctrinal statements, you should study Sections 17-55 of the Confession of Faith and questions 13-37 of the Catechism.

The third question regards the way the prospective member is determined to live personally. It does not ask if the member will promise to live a perfect life, but it does ask if he will "earnestly strive" to avoid those things that are evil and to grow both in knowledge and in spirit. If a person earnestly strives to do so, even when mistakes are made, he will keep on trying. But the most significant part of this question is whether the person will "live henceforth for Christ." This means that the church would like to know whether the person has a will to live the Christian life from this moment on. Again, this is not a question about perfection, but it is a question about determination and will. You might compare this question with Sections 56-74 of the Confession of Faith and questions 38-86 in the Catechism.

The fourth and fifth questions relate to the way in which the member is determined to live in relation to the congregation of which he wants to become a part. They have to do with cooperation, the use of the means of growth (such as worship and study), and the effort to get along together with other people in the church. The stewardship of time and possessions is one of the means of growth and cooperation which is specified. These questions can be compared with Sections 75-117 of the Confession of Faith and questions 87-105 of the Catechism.

In the fourth question one is also asked if he will "promise to abide by and support the rules and regulations of the Cumberland Presbyterian Church." This part of the question may be a bit confusing to some people, since there is no published set of rules and regulations to which we can point. The rules and regulations which are meant are the total of the matters on which we agree in the local church, presbytery, synod, and the General Assembly. They will change from time to time as the conditions may change. The purpose of the question seems to be to emphasize that the church does exist as a body, but it cannot do so unless the individual members work together according to the rules which are adopted. The rules are made by the session, which is the governing body of a congregation. They are also made by the presbytery, which has in it representatives from the local churches. They are also made to govern the whole church by the General Assembly, which passes its orders down to the presbyteries and through the presbyteries to the churches.

You will notice that these questions are "recommended" as the form of covenant into which members enter. If a session should desire to change the questions, they would have the right to do so, but would doubtless want to follow the general ideas suggested by the form. Those who affirm their faith and their intention to live the Christian life in keeping with this form are accepted as members of the church on what we call their "profession of faith." Having answered in the affirmative the questions which the session proposed to them, the persons who have not previously been baptized receive baptism as a "sign or symbol of the baptism of the Holy Spirit" which the believer claimed in answer to the second question. To us baptism is not the door into the church, as you will find more fully discussed in chapter 8, but is a part of the profession of faith which admits the member into the church.

Those who wish to unite with our church, having been members of some other Christian body, are received upon a letter of dismissal and recommendation from that body, or by transfer from those churches which do not make a practice of granting letters. This transfer is necessary in order to prevent the name of the member appearing on the roll of both churches. When the member wishes to change from the former church to our church, he is also asked to appear before the session and the session asks if in making this transfer he renews his vows to Christ and the church and transfers his allegiance to the new congregation of which he is to become a part. This question in fact is a summary and reaffirmation of the same things the individual said when he first joined the church.

We sometimes speak of this as "belonging to the church." This is a significant statement for it tells us why we do become members of the body of Christ. It is first of all because we "belong" to Christ and there is nothing else reasonable to assume but that we would be a part of his body. Paul once said that we are not our own but have been bought with a price. In this sense, all Christians belong to Christ and therefore to his body on earth. In Section 100, our Confession of Faith differs from the Westminster Confession, which says that outside the church "there is no ordinary possibility of salvation." Evidently those who wrote our Confession were trying to avoid the teaching that membership in the church saves the individual, but by omitting this statement, they did not imply that the truth is not there. If a person "belongs" to Christ, it is impossible for him not to be a part of his body.

This matter of "belonging" implies another very practical idea. If you have some object in your house, it "belongs" in a certain place. If it is somewhere else, it is not where it belongs. So it is with the children of God by faith. They belong in the body of Christ. This is where they should be and to be anywhere else is to be out of place. Thus, in this second sense, we become members of the church because we belong there.

Why Does the Church Exist?

This question has been partially answered in the preceding paragraph, but we need to look further at the mission of the church. Our Confession of Faith does not make a clear statement as to the mission of the church in so many words, or under such a title.

In Section 100 of our Confession of Faith it is stated that the church consists of those who have entered into a covenant with God and some organized body of Christians "for the maintenance of religious worship." Also in Section 101 we state that "Unto this visible church Christ has given the ministry, the word, and the ordinances for its edification." A thorough analysis of these statements can be taken as the mission of the church. It should not be assumed that the "maintenance of religious worship" limits the work of the church to what happens when the group gets together in the church building for what we call a religious service. This is certainly one of the functions of the church, but as was stated in Isaiah 6:11, the call of God which comes to us in worship has no limitations so long as there are human needs to be met. What happens in our worship of God is still in operation. This is what is meant by "the ministry" being given to the church. The church meets together for worship. It disperses for ministry.

We sometimes have difficulty in deciding what the purpose of the church is and express it by the statement that its purpose is "the winning of souls." This is certainly one of the objectives of the work of the church. The danger, however, in making this the limiting statement of the ministry of the church is that the winning of souls sometimes becomes a matter of counting numbers who have been won, or added to the roll. If the winning of souls includes all those matters asked in the questions contained in the form of church covenant, then this could justifiably be called the mission of the church.

Another statement which is sometimes used concerning the mission of the church is that it is for "the proclamation of the Word." This statement also can be limited or limitless. If the proclamation of the Word is taken to mean the preaching service or the revival meeting, then this is not the limit of the mission of the church. If, however, the proclamation of the Word is the total of the gospel, it might become the expression of Section 101 of our Confession. Then both the ministry and the ordinances would be included.

Another limitation on the ministry of the church which should be avoided might be deduced from the statement in Section 101 of our Confession when it says that these functions have been given to the church by Christ "for its edification." It is certainly true that, as our church covenant states, a part of the work of any Christian or body of Christians is growth in knowledge and spirit. This would be edification. But the purpose of the church is not limited to its own edification. The term edification carries with it the idea of building or improvement. This is a mission of the church. Sometimes people tend to ignore this in their effort to extend the work of the church to others. They then become missionaries to work on others, perhaps to the neglect of their own spiritual edification. It is given to the church to improve and grow not only in size and influence, but in strength of knowledge and character. But its improvement is not a selfish kind of improvement. The call which God gave to Abraham to "be a blessing" is still the call to the church. The mission of the church is not to the world outside the church alone, but it is to the whole man in the whole world, including those inside as well as those outside the church. If the church is edified by "the ministry, the word, and the ordinances" and "by his own presence in spirit" it cannot fail to perform its mission regardless of how the mission may be expressed in words.

The material in the remaining chapters of this book deal principally with our beliefs as a denomination. Not all sections of the Confession of Faith are included in the discussion, but those sections that have to do with the most controversial ideas are dealt with in brief. A complete study of the Confession of Faith, paragraph by paragraph, has been made in the book *We Believe and So We Speak* (by this author), to which the reader is referred.

SUBJECTS FOR FURTHER STUDY

1. Classify all the denominations with which you are familiar according to their form of government.
2. Make a more thorough study of Calvinism and Arminianism.
3. Put in outline form what you consider the distinguishing characteristics of the Cumberland Presbyterian Church.
4. What is the ecumenical movement? In what sense is our denomination an ecumenical group?
5. Study the sections of the Confession of Faith and the Catechism which are listed under the heading "How Do We Become Members of the Church?"
6. Make a thorough study of the questions suggested in our Form of Church Covenant.
7. Formulate a comprehensive statement concerning the nature and the mission of the church.

3

The Holy Scriptures

"The Holy Scriptures comprise all the books of the Old and New Testament which are received as canonical, and which are given by inspiration of God to be the rule of faith and practice.

"The authority of the Holy Scripture depends not upon the testimony of any man or church, but upon God alone.

"The whole counsel of God, concerning all things necessary for his own glory-in creation, providence, and man's salvation-is either expressly stated in the Scriptures, or by necessary consequence may be deduced therefrom; unto which nothing at any time is to be added by man, or from the traditions of men; nevertheless, we acknowledge the inward illumination of the Spirit of God to be necessary for the saving understanding of such things as are revealed in the Word.

"The best rule of interpretation of the Scriptures is the comparison of scripture with scripture" (Cumberland Presbyterian Confession of Faith, Sections 1-4).

"The reading of the Holy Scriptures of the Old and New Testament in the congregation is a part of the public worship of God, and ought to be performed by ministers and teachers in such a manner as that all may hear and understand" (Directory of Worship, Section 8).

How Many Books Do We Consider Canonical?

Quite often the religious teaching of our Confession of Faith is not contained in the plain statement, but must be inferred from some word or phrase which seems to be quite casual. For example, in this statement regarding the Holy Scriptures, we notice that we are taught to accept "all the books of the Old and

New Testament which are received as canonical." The reason for the insertion of this statement is simply that the Roman Catholic Church has more books in its Bible than we accept.

These books are not received as canonical, or standard books, and our church fathers stated in our confession that we should limit our idea of the inspired scriptures to the sixty-six books. Furthermore, this shows that we are different from the Jews and the Church of Christ in that the Jews accept only the Old Testament and the Church of Christ accepts only the New Testament.

On What Does the Authority of the Bible Depend?

Also, we are taught that "the authority of the Holy Scriptures depends not upon the testimony of any man or church, but upon God alone." In this statement we are saying that we are different from the Roman Catholic Church. We believe that the Bible is true, not because the pope says that it is true, or because some church council has said that it is true, but because we accept it as God's Word.

In the third place, we show ourselves to be distinct from the Jews and the Christian Scientists when we say that to this Bible, as we accept it, "nothing at any time is to be added by man, or from the traditions of men." Among the Jews, the saying of the rabbis seem to be of equal importance, and sometimes more so, than the expressions of the Scriptures. Among the Christian Scientists the words of Mary Baker Eddy occupy a place which often seems to be superior to that accorded the Scriptures. A Jewish rabbi has declared that his group regarded the sermons of a modem rabbi as truly inspired as the sermons of Isaiah or Jeremiah. We would not accept this idea of inspiration. We believe that the Bible has come to us in such a way that its words are more authoritative than teachings found outside the Bible.

There is nothing out of date about the Bible. It is the eternal Word of God, and that is eternal truth. But in what sense is the Bible the Word of God? Did God write it? Did God dictate it? Did he just tell men what to write?

In What Sense Is the Bible the Word of God?

The Bible is either the work of men or the work of God. If man made it, he should be able to make a better one today. We cannot say that man is going backward in intellect. The men who wrote the Bible lived in a small part of the world, and the majority of them did not travel extensively. They did not have the contact with the world about them that we have today through our modern inventions. They did not have the store of knowledge at the disposal of the modern student. They did not write at the same time, but probably wrote over a period of sixteen hundred years. However, in spite of these handicaps, the Bible as we have it is still looked upon as the most helpful book in the world, and the most harmonious document at the disposal of men.

If we can make it clear that the writers of the Bible were inspired by God, that they were taught and led by the Holy Spirit in their utterances as recorded in the Bible, that they taught the truth and nothing but the truth, that their teachings were without error, then we shall have in the Bible a court of final appeal to which we can go in any age and settle questions of doctrine and living.

But, if the writers of the Bible were inspired only in the sense in which Shakespeare, Browning, and many others were inspired, to the extent that their minds were made more keen to see truth than ordinary men, then we shall continually be confronted with the task of reorganizing the truth that they set down and re-adapting it to the changing times. We can be thankful that we do not have to be continually trying to correct mistaken ideas of the writers of the Bible, and worrying about how our descendants in turn will have to correct our mistakes in the way we have modernized the Bible.

How Does Inspiration Differ from Revelation?

It would probably help us to get our thoughts clear on the question of the inspiration of the Bible if we would make a distinction between inspiration and revelation. Our great poets were doubtless inspired, but we do not claim for them a divine revelation. It is true that the term inspiration means "a supernatural influence which qualifies men to receive and communicate divine truth," but we have used the term in such a variety of ways that we often lose the idea of the reception of divine truth. It is more of the idea of revelation which is taught in the Bible regarding the way truth was received by men.

What does the Bible teach regarding its inspiration? In II Timothy 3: 16-17, we are taught that "all scripture is given by inspiration of God, and is profitable for doctrine, for reproof, for correction, for instruction in righteousness: that the man of God may be perfect, thoroughly furnished unto all good works." Men who heard the Word from the lips of the apostles recognized them as the words of God instead of the words of men, as can be seen by First Thessalonians 2: 13, "For this cause also thank we God without ceasing, because when ye received the Word of God which ye heard of us, ye received it not as the word of men, but as it is in truth, the Word of God."

In support of the statement that the prophets did not speak their own message but the message of God, we have II Peter 1:21 which says, "The prophecy came not in old time by the will of man: but holy men of God spake as they were moved by the Holy Ghost." The case of Balaam is another proof of the method of inspiration. In Numbers 22:38 Balaam says to Balak, "Have I now any power at all to say anything? the word that God putteth in my mouth, that shall I speak." Paul makes it clear that at times he is saying things from his own conscience, and that at other times he is speaking the words which God spoke through him. In writing to the Corinthians he said, "Which things also we speak, not in the words which man's wisdom teacheth, but which the Holy Ghost teacheth" (I Corinthians 2:13).

Jesus testified to the eternal relevance of the Scriptures, as well as to their truth, when he said, "Verily, I say unto you, till heaven and earth pass, one jot or one tittle shall in no wise pass from the law, till all be fulfilled" (Matthew 5:18).

Are There Errors in the Bible?

The Scriptures, as originally revealed were without error. But what shall we say about the Bible as we have it today? It has passed through so many translations and has been copied by so many hands that there is the possibility that errors have crept in. It is to be remembered that we have today no original manuscripts either of the Old Testament or the New Testament, but only copies of copies.

Although many are telling us that the Bible contains many errors and contradictions, we can truthfully say that the Bible as we have it today is the inerrant word of God insofar as it is an accurate rendering of the original words of the Scriptures; and that it is, to all practical purposes, a thorough and accurate rendering of the original languages. There are, it is true, many variations, hundreds of them, in the manuscripts we possess; but by careful study of the variants scholars are able to find with marvelous accuracy what the original manuscripts said. A large number of the variations are of no significance whatever. There are no variants which affect significantly the doctrines of the evangelical churches of the world. The Scriptures as we have them today, translated into the English language, are to all practical purposes the inerrant Word of God, guiding us through this modern age, solving our problems, strengthening our walk, and filling us with hope for the future.

SUBJECTS FOR FURTHER STUDY

1. The books of the Bible and their division into groups, such as Law, History, Poetry
2. The meaning of the terms "canonical" and "apocryphal" books
3. The origin and growth of the translation of the Bible
4. The various modern translations of the Bible
5. Examples in the Bible itself of the "comparison of Scripture with Scripture"
6. The unity of the books of the Bible
7. The meaning of the statement. "The greatest enemy of the Bible is ignorance"
8. The character of the Bible as judged from a literary standpoint
9. The full meaning of accepting the Bible as the only infallible rule of faith and practice
10. The place of the Scriptures in worship (see Confession of Faith, Sections 75-78)

4

God the Father

"There is but one living and true God, a self. existent Spirit, infinite, eternal, and unchangeable in His being, wisdom, power, holiness, justice, goodness, and truth" (Cumberland Presbyterian Confession of Faith, Section 5).

When Jesus was having his last talk with his disciples, he told them that they had seen the Father. They did not understand what he meant; and Philip declared that, if Jesus would show them the Father, they would be satisfied. Jesus answered him by saying that, when they had seen him, they had seen the Father.

In like manner we need not be surprised if at times we become bewildered in the Christian life, and fail to understand all the mysteries of the kingdom. Questions will arise in the minds of all who think, and certainly of those who think about the infinite truths of God. It is not possible for man to comprehend God, nor is it possible to describe an infinite God in finite terms. For that reason many times the terms we use confuse us, and we are led astray from the truth.

How Can God Be Three Persons?

The question naturally arises as to how one God can be three and one at the same time. He cannot be three and one in the same sense, nor does the Bible teach that he is. But, how can he be three and one? An answer to that question is impossible, for this reason: God is Spirit, and physical numbers cannot describe spiritual beings. This much we can understand, however: there is but one God, and this one God makes himself known to us in three distinct persons-Father, Son and Holy Spirit. As we see God in Christ, as we see the wonderful providence and care of God the Father, and as we experience the leadership of

28

the Holy Spirit, we have no difficulty in believing in the Trinity.

The distinguishing characteristic of man is the fact that he will not let the question about God rest. The history of man may be thought of simply as his attempt to fathom the infinite. Therefore, we need not be surprised if within our lifetime we are not able to learn all there is to know about God. In this brief chapter we shall attempt to see some of the characteristics of God that will benefit us in our everyday living.

What Does Spirit Mean?

In talking to the woman of Samaria, Jesus gives us one of the great truths about the being of God. He tells her that "God is Spirit" (John 4:24). In some versions of the Bible that statement is rendered, "God is a Spirit," but there is no necessity for the article. There is no article in the Greek language, and it has to be supplied in places where it is needed to make sense. At this place there is no need for it. We might as well read, "God is a love" or "God is a light," as to say "God is a Spirit." The thing Jesus actually said was, "God is Spirit." He was describing God.

In another place he defines what he means by spirit. When he was talking to the disciples in the upper room after his crucifixion, Jesus said, "Behold my hands and my feet, that it is myself: handle me, and see; for a spirit hath not flesh and bones as ye see me have" (Luke 24:39). It is evident from these words that Jesus thought of spirit as being in direct contrast to a body.

To say that God is Spirit is to say that God is incorporeal, invisible reality; that he is not material, but immaterial and invisible, yet none the less real. This is made clear in the revelation which God made of himself to Moses. "Take ye, therefore, good heed unto yourselves for ye saw no manner of similitude on the day that the Lord spake unto you in, Horeb out of the midst of the fire; lest ye corrupt yourselves, and make you a graven image, the similitude of any figure, the likeness of male or female" (Deuteronomy 4:15, 16). The insistence of the prophets throughout the ages upon the worship of a God of Spirit in contrast to a God who can be visualized is also evidence of this fact. The childish conception of God as a big man with long, flowing white beard is almost impossible for us to leave; but if we are to get our thoughts higher than the childish level we must understand that God is Spirit.

As we think of God as Spirit, let us not think of him as something abstract. God is a being, a personality. That is to say, he is a being who knows, feels, loves, hears prayers, acts intelligently in our behalf, and enters a father-child relationship with us.

What Sort of Spirit Is God?

He is a personality distinct from the persons and things which he has created. The Bible often refers to him as a "living God" as distinguished from the first cause or the absolute which philosophers talk about. He is the God who sustains, governs, and cares for the world he has created. He shapes the whole history of the world; makes a path for his people; delivers, saves, and punishes. He has a direct, personal interest in the affairs of men.

Also, this personal being is infinite in all his attributes and powers. In I John 1:5 we are taught that God is Light. These words set forth the perfection of God: "In him is no darkness at all." That is to say, in him there is no darkness of sin, no darkness of error, no darkness of ignorance, no darkness of imperfection.

God is omnipotent. His power is not limited in any way. "Is there anything too hard for me?" (Jeremiah 32:27). Jesus said, "With God all things are possible" (Matthew 19:26). "God has all life, glory, goodness, and blessedness in himself; not standing in need of any creatures which he has made, nor deriving any essential glory from them; and has most sovereign dominion over them to do whatsoever he may please" (Cumberland Presbyterian Confession of Faith, Section 1).

This God is also omniscient. The psalmist assured us of this fact when he wrote, "Great is our Lord, and of great power; his understanding is infinite" (Psalm 147:5). Similar thoughts are expressed in 1 John 3:20 and Acts 15:18. We are told in the Psalms that he knows the number of the stars. In Matthew we are told that not a sparrow falls but that he knows it. The greatest and the least things are known unto him.

The Bible also teaches that this omniscient, omnipotent God is a God of holiness. "Be ye holy, for I am holy" (I Peter 1:16), implies a doctrine that is expressed all through the Bible. The entire Mosaic system of law was built upon it. The ordinances regarding the washing of pots and pans and ceremonial cleansings were designed to teach the concept of the holiness of God. If the people failed to get the lesson and gave attention only to the outward form, their error was not traceable to fault in the ordinance, but to the weakness of their own souls.

There is no thought in the Christian faith that needs more emphasis today than the doctrine of the infinite holiness of our God. The chief fault of the various cults that are being practiced in our land is in their failure to look upon God as holy. *The keystone in the arch of Christianity is the doctrine of God's holiness.*

Likewise, our God is an omnipresent God. The psalmist asked, "Whither shall I go from thy spirit? Or whither shall I flee from thy presence? If I ascend up into heaven, thou art there; if I make my bed in hell, behold, thou art there. If I take the wings of the morning, and dwell in the uttermost parts of the seas; even there shall thy hand lead me and thy right hand shall hold me" (Psalm 139:7-10). We think of God as being in heaven, and so he is. Jesus said, "I go to prepare a place for you. And if I go and prepare a place for you I will come again and receive you unto myself; that where I am there ye may be also" (John 14:2, 3). *But we must not think that God is in heaven and nowhere else.* There is another childish thought of ours that when we think of God or talk to God our eyes or thoughts must be directed upward. That is good, to keep us reminded that God is a God who is high and lifted up, elevated and pure. It is *not* good if it causes us to think that God is in the heavens, far removed from the affairs of men. God is everywhere. He is in all parts of the universe. In Him each individual lives and moves and has his being.

Finally, God is a God of love. We have certain sects of people today who carry this doctrine to the extreme in another line and distort the meaning of John when he wrote (I John 4:8) that God is love. They deny the personality of God and misconstrue this teaching so that it no longer is a characteristic of God, but an impersonal abstraction which is God. Instead of saying that God is love in the way that we believe it, they go to the limit of saying that love is God. They not only say that God is good, but that good is God. That is quite a different statement, as any person can reasonably see. You might as well say that since God is light, light is God.

What is plainly taught in this passage is that God is a being whose life and conduct are governed by the principle of love. This is taught by the life of Jesus, who said, "He that hath seen me hath seen the Father." His every act was an act of love. His coming was a message of love. "In this was manifested the love of God toward us, because that God sent his only begotten Son into the world, that we might live through him" (I John 4:9). Christ's life was no dazzling display of glory, but a simple life of loving service.

In the statement that God is "infinite, eternal, and unchangeable in His ..... justice, goodness," it seems that we are denying a doctrine held by the Calvinistic groups under the head, "Decrees of God." This doctrine, according to Cumberland Presbyterian belief, cannot be regarded as just or good.

How Does Our Belief in God as Father
Compare with That of Other Presbyterians?

E. B. Crisman, in his *New Origin and Doctrines of the Cumberland Presbyterian Church* (1877), says the following about doctrines (pp. 83-92):

"It is said by some that the Presbyterian Confession of Faith is not obnoxious to the objections which our fathers raised, and hence that they were not justifiable in urging the importance of the exception to the idea of fatality. There is but one way to settle his question-viz., by an appeal to the record. Therefore, attention is invited to the following quotations from that Confession of Faith:

" 'Chapter II, Sec. 3. By the decree of God, for the manifestation of His glory, some men and angels are predestinated unto everlasting life, and others foreordained to everlasting death.

"'Sec. 4. These angels and men, thus predestinated and foreordained, are particularly and unchangeably designed and their number is so certain and definite that it cannot be either increased or diminished.

" 'Sec. 5. Those of mankind that are predestinated unto life, God, before the foundation of the world was laid, according to His eternal and immutable purpose, and the secret council and good pleasure of His will, hath chosen in Christ, unto everlasting glory out of His mere free grace and love without any foresight of faith or good works, or perseverance in either of them, or any other things in the creature, as conditions, or causes moving him thereunto, and all to the praise of His glorious grace.'

"The above three sections certainly seem to teach the idea of fatality which is all that our fathers claimed, especially as it is distinctly stated, in Section 5, that this predestination is made without any foresight of faith or any other thing in the creature as conditions. If the accepting Christ by faith is not a condition of everlasting life, the rejecting him by unbelief is not a condition of eternal death; all of which contradicts the Bible.

" 'Chapter X, Sec. 1.' All those whom God has predestinated unto life, and those only, He is pleased, in His appointed and accepted time, effectually to call, by His Word and Spirit, out of that state of sin and death in which they are by nature, to grace and salvation by Jesus Christ.

" 'Sec. 2. This effectual call is of God's free and special grace alone, and not from anything at all foreseen in man, who is altogether passive therein, until being quickened and renewed by the Holy Spirit, he is thereby enabled to answer this call, and to embrace the grace offered and conveyed in it.'

"Here, it is taught, as plainly as words can teach, that men are altogether passive' in their salvation until regenerated. This our fathers did not believe, and would not accept.

" 'Sec. 3. Elect infants, dying in infancy, are regenerated and saved by Christ through the Spirit, who worketh when, and where, and how He pleaseth. So, also, are all other elect persons who are incapable of being outwardly called by the ministry of the Word.

" 'Sec. 4. Others not elected, although they may be called by the ministry of the Word, and may have some common operations of the

Spirit, yet they never come to Christ, and therefore, cannot be saved; much less can men, not professing the Christian religion, be saved in any other way whatsoever, be they ever so diligent to frame their lives according to the life of nature, and the law of that religion they do profess; and to assert and maintain that they may, is very pernicious and to be detested.'

"The two sections quoted above appear to teach, plainly, that only elect infants and idiots are saved. The latter part of Sec. 4 urges the impossibility of the salvation of a heathen, as also does the answer to Question 60 in the Larger Catechism:

" 'They who, having never heard the gospel, know not Jesus Christ, and believe not in Him, cannot be saved, be they ever so diligent to frame their lives according to the light of nature, or the laws of that religion which they profess.'

"On the supposition that God makes an unconditional election of some men to salvation, without any reference to faith or good works foreseen in them, as the Presbyterian Confession of Faith teaches, and that men are 'altogether passive' in salvation until regenerated as taught, by the same authority, Cumberland Presbyterians have never been able to see why, in making His sovereign and unconditional selections of 'altogether passive' creatures, He would entirely overlook heathen and 'foreordain' everyone of them to everlasting death. We cannot understand why, on such a supposition, there might not be elect heathen, infants, idiots, and adults in Christian communities. Infants and idiots no more 'hear the gospel and Christ' than heathen do. Nor are Cumberland Presbyterians prepared to affirm that heathen who 'have not the law,' but 'are a law unto themselves,' cannot be saved, much less are we willing to say that 'to maintain that they can is pernicious, and to be detested.'

" 'Larger Catechism, Answer 68. All the elect, and they only, are effectually called; although others may be, and often are, outwardly called by the ministry of the Word, and have some common operations of the Spirit, who, for their wilful neglect and contempt of all the grace offered them, being justly left in their unbelief, do never truly come to Christ Jesus.'

"When this language is considered in the light of the doctrine else where taught, that men 'altogether passive' until 'renewed by the Holy Ghost,' it at once becomes most objectionable. Because, if God, as a sovereign, 'renews' and effectually calls some who are in 'the neglect and contempt' of grace, and passes by others who are also in 'the neglect and contempt' of grace--in the same sin and condition-without any 'foresight of faith or good works,' the reflecting mind at once inquires, Why the discrimination? If leaving one in his sins is to the 'praise of God's glorious justice,' why would not the leaving of all in their sins be more to the 'praise of His glorious justice?' But we will notice this point: in another place.

"Let it be remembered the object in presenting these quotations from the Presbyterian Confession of Faith is to show that our fathers had just and sufficient reasons for making the reservation, in adopting it, 'so far as it is agreeable to the word of God,' and that a legitimate interpretation of the language does convey, to the ordinary mind, the 'idea of fatality.' Many other quotations of similar import might be given, but the above are sufficient to give the reader an idea of the system of doctrine to which our fathers objected, and to which we still object."

What Objections to Presbyterian Doctrines Do We Voice?

Crisman continues as follows:

"We will now state, succinctly, some of the points on which we object to the system of doctrine held by our Presbyterian brethren:

"1. We object to the date of the act of election. We believe that God knew, certainly, from eternity which particular men would be saved and which would be lost, and knew them by name; but not that He elected from eternity every particular man who should be saved, and foreordained every particular man who should be lost. We think the Bible is exceedingly clear in teaching that men are personally and individually elected to salvation when they believe, and at no other time. 'When ye believed, ye were sealed.'

"2. We object to the idea that election to salvation is not contingent, but is made without any references to 'faith or good works, or any other thing in the creature.' If this be true, then it would seem absurd to require men to accept Christ in order to obtain salvation, or to say 'he that believeth shall be saved.'

"3. We object to the doctrine that God has, 'for His own glory, unchangeably foreordained whatsoever comes to pass in time, especially concerning angels and men.' The fact that God has foreordained an event is incontrovertible evidence that He approves it. If, therefore, He has foreordained everything connected with the history of angels and men, He approves everything in history. This would take the frown off the countenances of God, and instead of His not being able 'to look upon sin with the least degree of allowance,' He would give it an approving smile. For Adam's sin and the sins which once 'repented him that he had made man,' He could entertain no condemnation. We prefer to believe that there are many events which God allows, not foreordains, to angels and men, in the exercise of the free agency with which he had endowed them. Such an event was the rebellion in heaven, and such the sin of Adam, and the numerous sins of his posterity. We do not believe, as some do, that God foreordained that man should sin in order that He might have a field in which to exercise His mercy, and a theater on which He could display the grandeurs of His grace. But we do believe that, man having sinned in the voluntary exercise of his free agency, God overruled the event, as He does many less important ones in our lives, and made it the occasion for the exercise of his mercy, and the theater on which He has displayed the noblest and grandest attributes of heaven.

"4. We object to the idea that men are passive, in the matter of salvation, until God 'quickens and renews them' and that He quickens and renews only those who are elected from eternity. If this were true and God 'quickens and renews' you and does not me, then you are saved outside of your agency, and I am lost outside of mine. God 'quickens and renews' the few, and consequently, they find the 'narrow way,' He does not 'quicken and renew' the many, and they, consequently continue to walk the 'broad road' to destruction. Some men's idea of justice may be such that they can say all this would be 'to the praise of the glory of His justice;' but with our views of justice, we are too conscientious to say any such thing.

"5. We object to the idea that some must be punished eternally, to display God's justice, and some must be saved to display His grace. We have great respect for venerable institutions, but must be allowed to say that the Westminster divines made a mistake in supposing that the plan of salvation would have been in vain had none been saved by it, and that God's justice could not be displayed if all were saved. This mistake led them into a serious difficulty. In the effort to overcome this difficulty, they incorporated into their system the idea to which we are now objecting. We hold that the plan of salvation through Jesus Christ would not have been in vain, though every one of Adam's race had refused to accept. It is a great system of divine wisdom, love, and justice, vindicating the eternal principles on which God's government is established-a system which has filled heaven with wonder and admiration, unfallen and redeemed intelligences everywhere with joy, and hell with consternation. Throughout eternity, it will stand in bold relief, vindicating to the universe, by its own abstract grandeur, the wisdom, love, and justice of God. All this it would have done had no man accepted it. Not less than this would it have done though no man had rejected it. The consummation of the prime work of the gracious conception was not contingent on man's rejecting or accepting. God's glory and its display, and the vindication of His character and government are not contingent on human volitions. Though every sinner had turned his back upon the plan of salvation, it would still have been eternally manifest that,

> God, in the gospel of his Son,
> Hath all his mightiest works undone.'

"The glory of God's justice is certainly as much displayed in the gracious and eternal salvation as in the eternal punishment of a sinner; and hence there is no necessity that some should be lost in order to vindicate the 'glory of His justice.'

"There is a little book called 'The Bible, Confession of Faith, and Common Sense,' in which the author attempts to reconcile the Presbyterian Confession of Faith with the Bible and common sense. On the subject of God's electing some men to salvation and reprobating others to eternal punishment, he uses the following illustration: 'A certain great king had ten rebellious provinces. They had all rebelled without provocation, and under the same circumstances. The king led out an army and subdued them. He then selected five provinces and pardoned them, to show his mercy. To the other five he meted out severe punishment, to vindicate the dignity and justice of his throne.' And the author concludes by saying that the 'five suffering provinces have no cause to complain, as they only get justice in receiving the punishment they deserve.' Now this is true; but cannot anyone see that that king is obnoxious to charge of partiality, at the least, and the five suffering provinces will always feel that they no more deserved punishment than the other five? But allow me to extend the above illustration to an analogy to the plan of salvation. Suppose when the ten provinces were conquered, some one, capable of doing it, had stepped in between them and the offended majesty, and had suffered sufficient to atone for the crime of the whole ten, and, while the king acknowledged that the suffering was sufficient to atone for the crime of all, he said to five, You shall have the benefit of this atonement, and to the others, you shall not-how much more glaring the partiality? And what would be the necessity for such a course? Had not the dignity and justice of the throne been amply vindicated by the suffering ofthe substitute? And now, when Christ has suffered sufficient to atone for the sin of the whole world, and thus fully vindicated and displayed the dignity and justice of divine government, pray tell us where is the necessity for some to be lost to display the 'glory of God's justice'? Under such circumstances, if God selects you to salvation and passes me by, or foreordains me to eternal punishment, when our sin is the same, as long as my present mental constitution continues, my heart and mind will constantly rebel against the discrimination which has been made, and rebel justly, even while I would acknowledge that I suffer only the punishment which my sin deserves.

"6. We object to the doctrine that Christ died only for a part of mankind. Here, we think, the Westminster divines got into another difficulty by another mistake-viz.: that if Christ had made provision to save all, then all would necessarily, be saved. To overcome this difficulty, they adopted this language: 'Christ DID in the fullness of time, die for the sins of the elect, and rise again for their justification.' We believe that the fact that provision is made in the gospel for all and offered to all is no reason to believe that all will be saved. If a benevolent king should prepare an ample feast for a thousand destitute subjects and invite the whole thousand to come, that fact would not secure the presence of all; and if five hundred should decline to come, still the king's benevolence would be as much manifested as though all had been present. It is repulsive to suppose that God has selected one man for whom he has appointed Christ to die, and another man by his side involved in the same sin and alike helpless, for whom Christ should not die. We prefer the doctrine so beautifully expressed in the Bible, that as many as were represented in the fall of the first Adam were represented in the atonement of the second. 'As in Adam all died, so in Christ all are made alive;' and on no other ground can we reconcile and adopt the great Bible doctrine of universal depravity. If all are provided, in Christ, with a remedy for representative sin, then we can see no wrong in involving all in the sin of a universal representative. But if some are not provided with such remedy, it would seem the height of injustice to involve them in, and condemn them for, a sin in which they had no agency. Instead of limiting the provisions of the gospel to a part of our race, we prefer that enlarged and liberal view which extends it not only to the whole of our race, but to fallen creatures everywhere in the universe. This view suggests that Christ Jesus met and defeated at Calvary the powers of darkness, in a contest, not simply for the mastery of our race, but of all intelligent races in creation."

What Did the Presbyterian Statement of 1903 Say?

As has been referred to previously, in 1903 the Presbyterian Church, U. S. A., did try to tone down its Calvinism by inserting a "declaratory statement," which is as follows:

"While the ordination vow of ministers, ruling elders, and deacons, as set forth in the Form of Government, requires the reception and adoption of the Confession of Faith only as containing the System of Doctrine taught in the Holy Scriptures, nevertheless, seeing that the desire has been formally expressed for a disavowal by the church of certain inferences drawn from statements in the Confession of Faith, and also for a declaration of certain aspects of revealed truth which appear at the present time to call for more explicit statement, therefore the Presbyterian Church in the United States of America does authoritatively declare as follows:

"First, With Reference to Section 111 of the Confession of Faith: That concerning those who are saved in Christ, the doctrine of God's eternal decree is held in harmony with the doctrine of His love to all mankind, His gift of His Son to be the propitiation for the sins of the whole world, and His readiness to bestow His saving grace on all who seek it. That concerning those who perish, the doctrine of God's eternal decree is held in harmony with the doctrine that God desires not the death of any sinner, but has provided in Christ a salvation sufficient for all, adapted to all, and freely offered in the Gospel to all; that men are fully responsible for their treatment of God's gracious offer; that His decree hinders no man from accepting that offer; and that no man is condemned except on the ground of his sin.

"Second, With Reference to Chapter X, Section 3, of the Confession of Faith, that it is not to be regarded as teaching that any who die in infancy are lost. We believe that all dying in infancy are included in the election of grace, and are regenerated and saved by Christ through the Spirit, who works when and where and how He pleases."

But it will be noted that this declaratory statement was put in the back of the Confession of Faith and was not to take the place of the real Confession. To Cumberland Presbyterians, that seems to be an attempt to carry water on both shoulders. Those who wish to remain Calvinistic are shown the statement of the Confession of Faith. Those who cannot believe such to be the act of a just and good Father are shown the declaratory statement. Thus, everybody is satisfied and nobody is able to say what the church teaches. A study of Sections 8 and 9 of our confession, as well as other sections which relate to man's salvation and the work of Christ, show clearly that Cumberland Presbyterians believe God to be just and good.

In 1931 the Presbyterian Church, U. S., added a section to their Confession, titled "A Brief Statement of Belief." This statement included a word concerning the doctrine of election which said practically the same thing as the one by the United Presbyterians, quoted above. But this revealing footnote to the statement should be considered: "The General Assembly of 1931 ordered that this statement be printed and bound with the Confession of Faith. By direction of the General Assembly of 1939, this 'Brief Statement' shall not be considered as an addition to, a substitute for, or an amendment to, the Confession Faith or Catechism, or any part thereof." The statements in Confession of Faith of this church are as they were in 1810.

SUBJECTS FOR FURTHER STUDY

1. The names of God in the Bible
2. Richard Beard's Lectures on Theology, Vol. I on the Existence God, the Nature of God, and the Trinity

3. The work of God in Creation, Confession of Faith, Sections 10, 11
4. The providence of God, Confession of Faith, Sections 12 to 16
5. The implications of the term "Father," which Jesus used for God
6. The development of the idea of God in history
7. The nature of the gods in the various religions today

5

God the Son and
God the Holy Spirit

"Jesus Christ, the only begotten Son of God, was verily appointed before the foundation of the world to be the Mediator between God and man, the Prophet, Priest, and King, the heir of all things, the propitiation for the sins of all mankind, the Head of His Church, the Judge of the world, and the Savior of all true believers" (Cumberland Presbyterian Confession of Faith, Section 27).

The Cumberland Presbyterian Church believes not only in God the Father; it believes as well in the divinity of Jesus and the reality of his presence in the world today in the person of the Holy Spirit. Here, again, is a statement of our Confession which means more than appears on the surface. In discussing the person of Jesus Christ, the statement that he is "the Savior of all true believers," undoubtedly refers to the objection of the church to the doctrine of fatalism. Sections 17 to 33 of our Confession of Faith show that our church teaches that all men are to look to Christ for salvation and that whosoever will may come to him and find him to be a Savior.

We do not wish to distinguish between Jesus and God in this chapter, but simply to present Jesus as the manifestation of God. Just as a word is the manifestation of an idea, so Jesus is the manifestation of God. "The Word was made flesh and dwelt among us . . . full of grace and truth" (John 1:14). "And the Word was God" (John 1:1).

Was Jesus Divine?
A few people are satisfied to regard Jesus as the greatest of human prophets; but to the immense majority of the believers in Christ, he is the divine Son of

God. Either he was divine or he was a great deceiver. A deceiver he could not. have been, because he founded the purest system of religion and morals that has ever been presented to the world.

What men think of Jesus in the twentieth century is valuable, but not as valuable as the opinion of men who saw him as he was-men who lived with him. What I may think about the message of Phillips Books or D. L. Moody is not as valuable as the opinions of the men who heard the messages and were convinced of the truth through them.

The men who lived with Jesus were convinced of his greatness, even though some of them were antagonistic to him. The opinions of these friends and enemies are worthy of our notice.

John began his gospel by declaring that Jesus was in the beginning. "In the beginning was the Word, and the Word was with God, and the Word was God. The same was in the beginning with God. All things were made by Him; and without Him was not anything made that was made" (John 1:1-3).

When the angel declared to Mary that she was to be the mother of the Messiah, he said, "The holy thing which shall be born of thee shall be called the Son of God" (Luke 1:35). Later, when the angels told the world of the coming of the Messiah, they said, "Unto you is born this day in the city of David a Savior which is Christ the Lord" (Luke 2:11).

When John the Forerunner was preaching in the wilderness, he said that the person who was coming after him was such a character that he, John, was not worthy to unloose his shoes. He was not worthy to perform even the lowliest service for Him. Later, when he saw Jesus approaching the place of his preaching, John said, "Behold the Lamb of God, which taketh away the sin of the world" (John 1:29).

Once when Jesus was preaching in the territory surrounding the Sea of Galilee, some devils came out of the tombs and cried out, "What have we to do with thee, Jesus, thou Son of God?" (Matthew 8:29).

When Jesus asked his disciples what men thought about him, and then what the disciples thought about him, Simon Peter replied for the Twelve, "Thou art the Christ, the Son of the Living God" (Matthew 16:16).

The Father himself testified to the divinity of Jesus at the time of his baptism when the voice from heaven said, "This is my beloved Son, in whom I am well pleased" (Matthew 3:17).

When Jesus stood before the high priest at his trial, the high priest asked him under oath to declare or deny that he was the Son of God, and Jesus acknowledged that he was (Matthew 26:63).

Doubting Thomas also recognized Jesus as the divine Son of God as he met him in the upper room after the resurrection. As this doubtful disciple was convinced of the reality of the resurrection, he cried out, "My Lord and my God" (John 20:28).

When Paul addressed his letter to the Romans, he said that this *Jesus* was declared to be the Son of God with power by the resurrection from the dead (Romans 1:4).

Surely, with all this evidence from those who were with Jesus, there can be no doubt concerning the divinity. The prophets told how he would come, and he fulfilled their prophecies. The angels cried out that he was divine, and men understood them. Saints who had looked for the coming of the Messiah recognized him, even as a baby, and paid tribute to him. Wise men came hundreds of miles in pursuit of their vision and did not suffer disappointment. God himself testified from heaven that he was genuine; Jesus claimed it; the devils acknowledged it; the disciples accepted it; his resurrection proved it, and his influence on the world since that time leaves no doubt as to the truth of the doctrine.

Yet there are many today who say that to acknowledge that Jesus was divine is to display our ignorance, for such a thing could not have been. Still, such ignorance is preferable to an arrogance that would put our opinion over against the plain statements of God, Jesus, angels and the greatest men who lived at the time of Jesus and who could qualify in any court of our land today as competent witnesses.

When Pilate had examined Jesus in an effort to find something wrong in his life, he had to acknowledge, "I find no fault in him." Pilate's wife came to him and said, "Have thou nothing to do with that just man." And even when Pilate was swayed by his desire of popularity with the crowd, he said, "I am innocent of the blood of this just person" (Matthew 27:24).

Judas betrayed his Lord for money, but he came back to the authorities and said, "I have sinned in that I have betrayed the innocent blood" (Matthew 27:4).

The centurion who presided at the crucifixion looked at Jesus on the cross and said, "Certainly this was a righteous man" (Luke 23:47).

The thief by the side of Jesus as they both were crucified said, "This man hath done nothing amiss" (Luke 23:41).

All of these competent witnesses, men who knew the facts, who had examined the life of Jesus, many of them with the purpose of finding fault, said that there was no fault in him. He was divine and perfect.

The first-century Jewish historian Josephus, in his *Antiquities of the Jews,* writes about the times of Jesus and says, "There was a man about this time, a wise man, if it be lawful to call him a man, for he was a doer of wonderful works."

Was Jesus Without Sin?

Peter described Jesus as One "who did no sin, neither was guile found in his mouth" (I Peter 2:22). Christ once suffered for sins, the just for the unjust" (I Peter 3: 18). John, who knew Jesus more intimately than did Peter, said, "Ye know that he was manifest to take away our sins; and in Him is no sin" (I John 3:5).

Not only was Jesus without sin, but he was without the consciousness of sin which exists in the holiest men according to their holiness. The general opinion of men has been that holiness and sinlessness are impossible. Demosthenes attributed it to the gods alone. Cicero had never heard of or found a perfectly wise man. Mahomet records in the *Koran* that God commands him to pray for the forgiveness of sins. Buddha is not represented as having been sinless at first, but as having gradually attained it. Socrates detected in his heart all the germs of vice. Moses was guilty of sin. Isaiah was a man of unclean lips. St. Peter went off and wept tears of repentance. St. Paul confessed the himself the chief of sinners. John said, "If we say that we have no sin, we deceive ourselves, and the truth is not in us" (I John 1:8).

Jesus, on the other hand, never recognized in himself the least moral blemish. He was the personification of moral perfection. He invited, "Come unto me and I will give you rest." "Take my yoke upon you and learn of me" (Matthew 11:28, 29). Such claims as these could not have come from a sinner to his fellow sinners. We have, therefore, in Jesus the unique case of a man of unexampled holiness, and without any consciousness of sin. This harmonizes with and suggests the belief that the personality of Jesus was more than human, that it was divine.

What Are Other Evidences of Jesus' Divinity?

The miracles also testify to his divinity. From human nature we expect works within human capacity; from superhuman nature, works of superhuman capacity. The ministry of Jesus was full of mighty works which exceed human capacity, and which can be regarded as being no less than miraculous. Not the least of these miracles are the resurrection and the ascension of Jesus. They form the climax of a superhuman life.

Christ's influence on the world proves his divine origin. Enumerate all the great men who have ever lived, whether kings, conquerors, statesmen, patriots, poets, philosophers, or men of science, and their influence for good will be found as nothing compared to that exerted by *Jesus*. He who was in outward form a Galilean peasant, who died a malefactor's death, has founded a kingdom which has endured for centuries and shows no signs of decay. Commencing with the smallest beginnings, it has embraced all the progressive races of men. Those by whom it has not been accepted are in a state of stagnation and decay.

The argument from Christian experience is in some ways the least compelling when put down on paper or spoken from the stand, but it is in reality the strongest of all the arguments for the divinity of Jesus. Men who have found God *through* Christ do not have any difficulty in seeing God *in* Christ. What keeps men Christian and adds to the number of Christian converts is the fact that he really does give to his followers the peace, joy and communion with God, and victory over sin that he said he would give. Those who come to Jesus in faith do not find him wanting. Their characters are transformed, and they thereby become capable of acts that, without him, they never would have attempted. Laboring and heavy laden, they go to their Lord and in him first rest unto their souls.

Why should anyone doubt the divinity of Jesus? It seem that the record of the life and work of Jesus would be sufficient to convince any person that he is more than a man.

What difference does it make whether we believe in his divinity? If we doubt his divinity, then we must doubt his truthfulness; for he stated and implied that he was divine. If we doubt his truthfulness, then we must doubt all that he said and all that he can mean to mankind. This, of course, will destroy the whole Christian religion and man's hope for salvation. On the other hand, if we believe in his divinity, we not only believe what he said about himself and about us, but we shall be inspired by the thought that we have in him one who is supremely able "to save them to the uttermost that come unto God by him."

What Do We Believe About the Holy Spirit?

"The Holy Spirit, operating through the written word, and through such other means as God in His wisdom may choose, or directly, without means, so moves upon the hearts of men as to enlighten, reprove and convince them of sin, of their lost estate and of their need of salvation; and, by so doing, inclines them to come to Christ" (Cumberland Presbyterian Confession of Faith, Section 39).

It is significant that our Confession of Faith has very little to say in plain terms about the doctrine of the Holy Spirit. This is undoubtedly due to the lack of controversy and dispute over the doctrine. There is, however, in later days a great deal of necessity for this doctrine. The statements which our Confession of Faith does make show that we differ in this particular from such groups as the Christian churches, which deny the operation of the Holy Spirit, and the Unitarian Church, which denies the existence of the Trinity. While we believe in one God, we assuredly believe that he is present in the world today in the form of the Holy Spirit.

Anyone who knows God the Father and the Son, but who does not know God the Holy Spirit, has not attained unto the Christian conception of God. Furthermore, anyone who does not know the Holy Spirit as a person has not attained to a well-rounded Christian experience. At first thought, it may seem that the doctrine of personality of the Holy Spirit is a purely technical and impractical doctrine, but it is not, as we shall see later.

Why Is It Important to Believe In the Holy Spirit as a Person?

The doctrine of the personality of the Holy Spirit is important from the standpoint of worship. If the Holy Spirit is a person, as he is, and if we do not know him as such; if we think of him as an impersonal force or influence, then we are robbing a divine person of the worship, the confidence, love, and surrender which belong to him.

Theoretically we all worship the Holy Spirit. Every time we sing the Doxology we ascribe praise to the Holy Spirit. *But it is one thing to worship theoretically, and quite another to worship actually.* It is one thing to sing words, and quite another to understand and mean these words.

The doctrine of the personality of the Holy Spirit is important from a practical standpoint also. If we think of the Holy Spirit as a mere influence, then our thoughts will be, "How can I get hold of the Holy Spirit and use it?" But if we are thinking of the Holy Spirit as a person, we shall be thinking, "How can the Holy Spirit get hold of me and use me?" If we think of the Holy Spirit as an influence, we shall be thinking, "How can I get more of the Holy Spirit?" If we think of the Holy Spirit as a person, we shall be saying, "How can the Holy Spirit get more of me?" If you think of the Holy Spirit as an influence, you will find yourself strutting around boasting that you have more of the power than your neighbors. On the other hand, there is no doctrine in the Bible which makes us more humble than that of the Holy Spirit as a person who takes up his abode in our hearts and takes possession of our lives.

All the distinctive marks or characteristics of personality are ascribed to the Holy Spirit in the Bible. Knowledge, feeling, and will are the distinctive characteristics of personality. A person does not have to have a body. Hands, feet, eyes, and ears are not marks of personality, but marks of corporeity.

"But all these worketh that one and the self-same Spirit, dividing to every man severally as he will" (I Corinthians 12:11). Here will is ascribed to the Holy Spirit. The thought clearly is that the Holy Spirit is not a divine power that we get hold of and use according to our will, but that *the Holy Spirit is a person who gets hold of us and uses us according to his will.* That point is fundamental, for a number of people today are striving to get superhuman power to use in their lives. What could we do with superhuman power? What evil we could produce!

"And he that searcheth the hearts knoweth what is the mind of the Spirit" (Romans 8:27), is a passage that indicates that the Holy Spirit has a mind.

The passage, "Now I beseech you, brethren, for the Lord Jesus Christ's sake, and for the love of the Spirit" (Romans 15:30), indicates that the Spirit is not a force, but a Person who loves us. We kneel down to pray to God the Father, thanking him for the love that he has for us; we thank God for the love of Jesus Christ. But how many times have we ever thanked God for the love of the Holy Spirit? Yet, *if it had not been for the love of the Holy Spirit, there would be no salvation for us!* The love of the Father caused Jesus Christ to come into the world; the love of Christ caused him to die for us, and the love of the Spirit causes him to follow us all the days of our lives and continually try to get us to accept the love of God.

"Grieve not the Holy Spirit of God" (Ephesians 4:30), is a passage which teaches that the Spirit is a person whose feelings can be hurt. Can you grieve matter, force, influence? If we could ever get fixed in our minds the truth that the Holy Spirit is grieved by our sins, it would keep us in many times of temptation.

The actions that are ascribed to the Holy Spirit indicate that he is a person. The Holy Spirit is said to search the deep things of God, to pray, to teach, to act asa comforter, an advocate, a counsel. When Jesus said, he would send another Comforter, he implied that the Comforter would be the sort of helper that he had been: He was to take the place of Jesus in the lives of the disciples.

These truths should be a cure for fear, loneliness, lack of confidence and broken-heartedness. With the Holy Spirit by our side, nothing is too hard or too big for us to undertake.

What Can the Holy Spirit Do?

What are the four things that the Holy Spirit does for every soul that only the Holy Spirit can do?

First, the Holy Spirit saves our souls. There is no other way to get into the kingdom of heaven except through regeneration by the Holy Spirit. As Jesus talked to Nicodemus, he told him that, in addition to his natural birth, he would have to experience the birth of the Spirit. Jesus was not adding to the already-overburdened ritual of his day; he was simply setting forth the one requirement of getting into the kingdom. There are too many examples on record indicating that no other agency is used in the conversion of men for this necessary work of the Holy Spirit to need any repetition here.

Second, the Holy Spirit teaches men. He opens our eyes to spiritual truth. The entrance of the Holy Spirit is like turning on the light in a dark room. One of the great works of the Spirit in this capacity comes to us when we are reading our Bible. It has been the common experience of men to read a passage several times; and then suddenly, as if from some mysterious realm, a new light comes upon that passage that we had never dreamed of before. It was not reason that brought it; it was not anything else that you can satisfactorily explain, except the teaching work of the Holy Spirit.

Third, the Holy Spirit guides men in the patterning of their Christian lives after that of Christ. This process of development, of growth in grace, is accomplished only as we allow the Holy Spirit, who knows the way of life, to guide our thoughts, words, and actions, as well as our ideals.

Fourth, the Holy Spirit acts as a comforter, which truly means one who fills us with strength. Comfort is not a weak soothing of the feelings, as we ordinarily use the word, but is a strong term representing an active, courageous spirit. It is this Comforter who enabled the martyrs to face death for the cause of Christ; who inspires young men and old to undertake difficult tasks in the name of the Master; who gives determination to all to stand for the right in the face of all the opposition of evil.

There is little wonder, then, that Jesus said in his last talk with his disciples before his ascension, "Tarry ye in the city of Jerusalem, until ye be endued with power from on high" (Luke 24:49).

SUGGESTIONS FOR FURTHER STUDY

1. The necessity for the coming of Christ. Sections 17-33 of the Confession of Faith
2. Other declarations of Jesus regarding his divinity
3. Other evidences of the divinity of Jesus in and out of the Bible
4. The Old Testament prophecies which were fulfilled in the person and work of Jesus
5. The figures of speech in the Bible describing Jesus, such as "Great Physician," "The True Vine," "Rock of Ages," and "Lamb of God"
6. The conception of God which Jesus emphasized in his life and work
7. The meaning of Galatians 4:4
8. The passages in which Jesus referred to God
9. The account of the coming of the Holy Spirit, Acts 2
10. The names given to the Holy Spirit in the Scriptures
11. The distinction between the three persons in the Trinity shown at the baptism of Jesus
12. The prominence given to the Holy Spirit in the work of the early Christian Church
13. The history of Pentecost before and after Christ
14. The subject of Divine Influence, with Scripture references, in the Confession of Faith, Sections 38-41
15. The work of the Holy Spirit as taught in John 16:8

6

Regeneration, Justification, Sanctification

"Those who believe in the Lord Jesus Christ are regenerated, or born from above, renewed in spirit, and made new creatures in Christ" (Cumberland Presbyterian Confession of Faith, Section 51).

What Is Regeneration?

Many times we glibly repeat passages of scripture in our meetings or in our Sunday school without any definite idea as to their meaning.! Down deep in our hearts we have not considered their meaning. As with certain words that are used every day, we could not give a clear definition of them. That is true with the verse that we repeat, "Except a man be born again, he cannot see the kingdom of God" (John 3:3). We have an idea of its meaning; but when we attempt to tell others what it means to be born again, we cannot make ourselves understood.

The writer of Second Peter 1:4 gives us a clear definition of the new birth in these words: "Whereby are given unto us exceeding great and precious promises; that by these ye might become partakers of the divine nature, having escaped the corruption that is in the world through lust. If we accept the truth of these words, we must admit that the new birth is the impartation of a new nature, God's own nature, that we have received through his great promises. According to Colossians 3:10, the regenerated man is "renewed in knowledge

48

after the image of him that created him." He feels as God feels, loves the things God loves, hates things God hates, wills as God wills. He has gone through a thoroughgoing change in the deepest springs of thought, feeling, and action. So true is this that Paul could say, "If any man be in Christ, he is a new creature (creation): old things are passed away; behold all things are become new" (II Corinthians 5: 17).

Is Regeneration Necessary?

Our Confession of Faith teaches that regeneration is necessary to every person who comes into the world because in every human heart there is enmity against God (Section 52). This statement denies the doctrine that it is possible for a child to be brought up in such a perfect environment that he will never need regeneration. We believe that there are certain things which we can do to help people to accept Christ. What we may do corresponds to the preparation of soil for seed. But we also believe that there must be a germ of life which no outside influence can provide and which is not present in the natural state of man. It is easy to see that a child brought up in a perfect environment would have quite a different experience from one who does not have this environment, just as a field may be kept free from weeds. But it is also easy to see and to experience the hard truth that in every human heart there is a tendency toward evil which must be overcome by something outside one's self.

How Does It Differ from Conversion?

In ordinary conversation we use the words "conversion" and "regeneration" interchangeably, but there is a distinction between regeneration and mere conversion or moral reform. This reform is an outward thing, a turning around. One is faced the wrong way; he turns and faces the other way. His better judgment, or the advice of friends, or a number of other things may cause him to realize that he should turn in the other direction. *Regeneration, however, is not a mere outward change, but a change in the deepest depths of one's being that is produced by the power of the Holy Spirit,* and then shows itself in a life in keeping with the inward change. Many an apparent outward conversion is a temporary thing, because it did not go deep enough; but regeneration is a permanent thing. When man becomes a partaker of the divine nature, that divine nature becomes a permanent, abiding reality in the man. A man may be reformed a hundred times, but he can be regenerated but once.

What Comes of Regeneration?

What are some of the results of this experience of regeneration? There are many that we do not have space to consider, but certainly one of the outstanding results is the fact that then *man becomes in reality and truth the dwelling place of the Holy Spirit.* "Know ye not that your body is the temple of the Holy Ghost which is in you, which ye have of God?" (I Corinthians 6:19).

That indwelling Spirit does things for the individual that he could not do for himself, and which could not be done for him by others.

Another result of the new birth is that our lives are transformed by the renewing of our minds so that we are no longer fashioned according to the things of the world (Romans 12:2). Of course, the regenerated man does not begin to manifest perfectly at once that which he has as a germ within himself. He begins the spiritual life as he began the natural life, as a babe, and must grow and develop into manhood. It is irrational and unwarranted by Scriptures to suppose that the minute a man is born into the kingdom he has no more troubles spiritually and that he is a full-grown spiritual being, able to understand the mysteries of God and to do all the difficult things of the spiritual life. But from the moment he is born into the kingdom, he has in germ all the moral perfection that is to be his when he is fully grown spiritually.

Another result of the new birth is one that is not clearly understood when we read the passage upon which it is founded. I must confess that I have read it many times and trembled because I thought it meant something else from that which understand it to mean now. "Whosoever is born of God doth not commit sin; for his seed (that is, God's seed) remaineth in him; and he cannot sin, because he is born of God" (I John 3:9). That passage means just what it says, if we take into consideration the force of the words and the tense of the verbs. First of all, let us see what the word "sin" means.

John has been careful to define it for us in the words of the context. By his definition, what he is thinking of as sin is doing something, not merely leaving something undone, and not merely sinful thoughts and desires. In verse 4 he says sin is the transgression of the law. This is not to say that there is no other idea of sin in the Bible, but we have no right to bring in other meanings in dealing with John's statement, since he has been careful to define it for us; and his definition is that sin is lawlessness; that is, such acts as reveal conscious disregard of the will of God as revealed in the Bible. Sin as here used means a conscious and intentional violation of the laws of God. The regenerated man will not be doing that which he knows to be contrary to the will of God. He may do that which is contrary to God's will; but which he does not know to be contrary to God's will; but that does not constitute lawlessness. When he finds out that his actions are not in keeping with God's will, he will repent.

Furthermore, the tense of the verb has something to do with the meaning. In this context, the present tense of the verb implies continuous action. *It is not taught here that one born of God never sins in a single act, but that he will not go on sinning continually, will not make a deliberate practice of sin.* His daily practice is the doing of righteousness.

"If any man be in Christ, he is a new creation; old things are passed away; behold, all things are become new." In the place of old ideas, old affections, old purposes and old choices, are new ideas, new affections, new purposes and new choices. He is a new man.

How Does Regeneration Take Place?

Naturally, the question arises as to how we may become such new creations. A sound scriptural basis for regeneration is repentance and faith.

Before John came, the prophets preached that men should repent. When he came, he said, "Bring forth fruits meet for repentance" (Matthew 3:8). Jesus followed him with the same message of repentance. He sent his disciples out to preach the same message. But many people have a confused idea as to what it means to repent. There are many who do not claim to be Christians today simply because they have been misled on the subject of repentance.

Instead of taking God's words and showing to the sinner the way of eternal life, many times workers will try to explain the way in their own words and experiences. It is certain then to be only man's wisdom, and the one who is seeking Christ gropes around blindly wanting to be a Christian, but not knowing how.

One day in a revival meeting, there was a young man left at the altar after the services. He plainly showed that he was troubled. Someone approached him and asked if he had found Christ. He replied that he had not and that he considered it all a great mystery. Upon being asked why it appeared to be such a mysterious thing, he replied that he could not be a Christian until he had experienced the things that others had. They asked him to what experiences he referred, and he said, "A lady just told me how she got Christ, and I have not had any of those signs at all."

When there are such plain, clear explanations of what it means to come to Christ, and exactly how to come, why should we try to take the matter in our own hands and try to lead souls to Christ through a duplication of our particular experience? *The apostles preached repent, once, and men were born into the kingdom.*

Evangelist Gipsy Smith said, "Repentance is not promising to be better. There are plenty of people who have been promising to be better ever since they can remember. When God laid his hands on them, they were ready to promise everything, but as soon as the hand was lifted the promises were broken, and the promiser was farther away from God than before.

"Repentance is not crying. It is not excitement. It is not emotion. It is not kneeling down and groaning. It is not going to hear preachers deliver sermons. Jesus tells us what it is in the illustrations he gives as recorded in Luke's Gospel, the fifteenth chapter. The sheep was lost without any intention of its own, but it was lost. The silver was lost in the house through somebody's carelessness. The son was lost through his own will. He was a prodigal before he left home. He was a rebel before he received a penny of his money.

"When the sheep went astray, a man went after it. When the silver was lost, a woman went after it. When the son went astray nobody went after him. If his father had gone after him and had brought him back, against his will, he would have been a prodigal still. He went astray, took every step of his own will, and he had to come back every inch of the way of his own will. He didn't write a letter asking his father to send a chariot for him; he didn't ask others to give him a lift; he walked back with bleeding feet and an aching heart."

It is when a man has learned that his own sin has banished him from his father's house; that his own sin pits him with the swine of the earth; when his sin reminds him of his home forsaken; when he realizes that God is not a despot, not a cruel executioner, but a loving father yearning for his wandering children-then it is that he has changed his mind concerning sin.

An evangelist in Glasgow went from church to church for ten weeks, preaching for a week at each of the various churches. He noticed that one man followed him to all the services for seven weeks. One night the evangelist and the man were left alone after the service, and they began to talk. As the evangelist was trying to show the man the way of salvation, a third party stepped up and asked for the privilege of talking to the sinner. When his request was granted, the third man told the sinner to read John 3:16. "Do you believe that?" he asked. "I do," replied the man. "Then read Romans 10:9, about confessing with the mouth and believing with the heart." The man said that he believed that, too. Then the third man said, "Well, you are a Christian." The sinner, however, denied and said, "You have read to me. Now let us read one of my choice." They read Isaiah 55:7, "Let the wicked forsake his way," "Now," said the sinner, "I am that unrighteous man. I have not forsaken my way and my unrighteous thoughts, and I am not a Christian. In my heart is a great sin, and I know I cannot be saved until I surrender it."

This is a sermon on repentance. *Not until the unrighteous man has come to regard sin as something that he will have no more of has he repented of sin.*

Abandonment of sin is but a part of the way of the regenerated life. The way of salvation is the way of faith. "Believe on the Lord Jesus Christ and thou shalt be saved" is a verse of Scripture that has led many to a knowledge of a new way.

One day a group of soldiers were in the lobby of a hotel engaging in a corrupt conversation; and then, as if by magic, the conversation drifted to the subject of salvation. One corrupt soldier said, "I expect to be saved." The whole group was surprised, and they asked him why. "The Bible says," he explained, "that if we believe on the Lord Jesus Christ we will be saved, and I certainly believe on Jesus.

It would be interesting to know exactly what his conception of belief in Jesus Christ was. Probably he had the same idea that a number of people have: that, if he believed a certain number of facts about Jesus, he would be saved. If he believed that Jesus was born in a manger in Bethlehem, was brought up in Nazareth, had a public ministry of three years, was crucified, buried, and rose again after three days, he probably thought he had satisfied the requirements. *That is believing about Jesus, but believing on Jesus is something vastly more than that.*

In John 1:12 the words "receive" and "believe" are used as synonyms. According to that verse, believing on Jesus is receiving him into the life, enthroning Jesus in the center of our being. It is not merely believing certain facts about him.

Galatians 2:20 and Revelation 3:20 both express the thought that faith is letting Christ take possession of the heart. Dr. F. B. Meyer, when a young man, heard the voice of God saying to him, Give me the keys to your heart." He offered the keys but tried to keep one back for himself. The voice came the second time with the same result. On the third time he replied, "Here they all are, the little key and all, take them and come in to cleanse the house and take absolute possession of my life. That is faith: putting the keys into the hands of the Master.

"That we should be to the praise of his glory, who first trusted in Christ. In whom ye also trusted after that ye heard the word of truth, the gospel of your salvation; in whom also after that ye believed ye were sealed with that Holy Spirit of promise," reads Ephesians 1: 12, 13. In this passage the words "believe" and "trust" are used synonymously. If we define faith by that message, we should say that believing in Christ is trusting Christ. We use the word believe in that sense frequently. We say, "I believe in that man." We mean that we are willing to trust him, and not that we simply know something about him.

"I know whom I have believed, and am persuaded that he is able to keep that which I have committed unto him against that day" (II Timothy 1:12). This verse marks the climax of the progression of faith in the two previous verses. First, we learned to know the Lord Jesus. We could not believe on him until we knew him. Second, as we learned about him, even in childhood, we were beginning to trust him. Then, as the final step in our faith, we committed ourselves to him. "Faith cometh by hearing, and hearing by the word of God" (Romans 10: 17).

Jesus said, "As Moses lifted up the serpent in the wilderness, even so must the Son of Man be lifted up; that whosoever believeth in Him should not perish, but have eternal life" (John 3:14). The first was a look-and-live salvation, and so also is the second. Look and live, my brother, live!"

What Is Justification?

"All those who truly repent of their sins, and in faith commit themselves to Christ, God freely justifies; not by infusing righteousness into them, but by pardoning their sins and by counting and accepting their persons as righteous; not for anything wrought in them, but for Christ's sake alone; not by imputing faith itself, or any other evangelical obedience, to them as their righteousness, but by imputing the obedience and satisfaction of Christ unto them, they receiving and resting on him and his righteousness by faith.

"Justification is purely of God's free grace, and is a full pardon for all sins, and exemption from all their penal consequences; but it imparts no moral qualities or merits to the believer, being strictly a legal transaction. Though of free grace alone, it is conditioned on faith, and is assured to none but penitent and true believers, who being justified, have peace with God through our Lord Jesus Christ" (Cumberland Presbyterian Confession of Faith, Sections 48 and 49).

The distinctive doctrine of the Protestant churches is the doctrine of justification by faith. Though it is fully set forth in the doctrines of Paul, it is a doctrine which runs through the whole Bible. In the very first book of the Bible, we are taught that Abraham's faith won for him the proper relationship with his God.

In What Two Ways Is This Doctrine Viewed?

In general there are two opposing views of how men are justified. *One view is that men are justified by their own works,* i.e., on the ground of something they do for themselves. These good works may be their moral conduct, or their keeping of the Golden Rule, or something of that sort. It may be work of a religious nature, such as doing certain amounts of penance, saying prayers, joining the church, being baptized, taking communion, or the performance of religious duties. *The other view is that men are justified not by their own works, but entirely by the works of Another,* and that all men have to do with it is to appropriate that justification to themselves by trusting in him who is the atonement-who brings men into harmony with the Father.

It is plainly stated in Romans 3:20 that by the deeds of the law no person is justified, for the law is designed to bring us to a knowledge of our sins. The law does not bring purification, but makes us realize the need of that purification. "The law is a schoolmaster to bring us to Christ" (Galatians 3:24). "The law came by Moses, but grace and truth by Jesus Christ." Romans 3:24 states that we are justified freely by his grace through the redemption that is in Jesus. If we believe this passage, then we accept the truth that justification is a gift that God gives to men absolutely without pay. The channel through which that gift comes is the redemption that Christ paid. "Christ hath redeemed us from the curse of the law, being made a curse for us" (Galatians 3:13). Who his own self bare our sins in his own body on the tree" (I Peter 1:24).

The one and only ground for justification is the shed blood of Jesus Christ. Of course, this doctrine is not accepted by the free thinkers of our day because they cannot explain it on natural grounds, but it is the only doctrine taught in the Bible, and the only one that the Old Testament prophets knew anything about. Isaiah taught it several centuries before Christ when he wrote, "All we like sheep have gone astray. . . and the Lord laid on him the iniquity of us all" (Isaiah 53:6).

God asks nothing else of the sinner but that he should believe on His Son, Jesus Christ; and when he does that, the sinner is justified. The question is not how much the sinner has done to deserve the favor of God, but whether he believes on him who justified the ungodly. There is feeling connected with the justified relation, but it is not a question of how the sinner may feel.

The Reverend John McNeill had been a ticket agent for a railroad, and a sinner. Then one day, in his perplexity, he wrote his pastor a letter asking him to explain the account of the conversion of the Philippian jailor (Acts 16:31). In his letter he told the pastor that he believed every word of the Bible, but did not feel any different. The pastor replied with a letter in which he said, "Did the passage say, 'Believe on the Lord Jesus Christ and you will have a glorious feeling?' No. It says 'Believe on the Lord Jesus Christ and thou shalt be saved.'"

Works have nothing to do with our salvation except to hinder it when we *trust in them.* The blood of Jesus Christ secures it, faith in Christ appropriates it. We are justified not by our works, but by his work. However, there is another side to the truth, and if our doctrine is to be completely balanced, we must look at that, too. In Romans 10:9, 10, we are taught, "If thou shalt confess with thy mouth the Lord Jesus and shalt believe in thine heart that God raised him from the dead, thou shalt be saved; for with the heart man believeth unto righteousness, and with the mouth confession is made unto salvation." The Apostle Paul here tells us that the kind of faith that justifies is the kind that comes from the heart, the kind that produces a life in keeping with the faith. What does it profit a man if he says he has faith, but has no works! James tells us that we can show our faith by our works.

Someone has said, "We are justified by faith without works, but we are not justified by a faith that is without works." *The faith that God recognizes is a faith that is invariably accompanied by good works.* The proof to us of the faith is the works, and we know that he who does not show his faith by his works has not found justifying faith. "We are justified by faith alone, but not by faith that is alone."

"Good works are such only as God has commanded in His word, and not such as may be devised by men out of blind zeal, or any pretense of good intention.

"Those who, in their obedience and love, attain the greatest height in this life, still fall short of that perfection which the Divine law requires; yet their good works are accepted of God, who, looking upon them in His Son, is pleased to accept and reward that which is sincere, although accompanied with many weaknesses and imperfections" (Cumberland Presbyterian Confession of Faith, Section 58, 59).

This part of our doctrine shows that we believe that God looks with favor upon our good deeds when they are sincere; but He does not justify us on the basis of our deeds.

Is Justification the Same as Forgiveness?

What is this thing we call justification? Is it the same as forgiveness? No, it is not. Forgiveness is negative, the putting away of sin. Justification is positive, the attitude of God toward the one forgiven. The believer is so united to Christ that God looks on him as being hid with Christ. God sees us not as we are in ourselves, but as we are in Him, and reckons us as righteous as he is. In other words, when a man accepts this saved relation, his old account is wiped out and God looks upon him as a new creature. No matter how bad and how black this account has been, the moment he believes in Jesus Christ that old record is wiped out. God then has absolutely nothing that he holds against that man. Even though the man is still imperfect and immature he is perfectly just in the sight of God. His present "state" may be imperfect, but his present "standing" in the sight of God is perfect. "There is, therefore, now no condemnation to them which are in Christ Jesus" (Romans 8:1). "By him all that believe are justified from all things, from which ye could not be justified by the law of Moses" (Acts 13:39).

What is Sanctification?

"Sanctification is a doctrine of the Holy Scriptures, and it is the duty and privilege of believers to avail themselves of its inestimable benefits, as taught in the Word of God. A state of sinless perfection in this life is not authorized by the Scriptures, and is a dogma of dangerous tendency" (Cumberland Presbyterian Confession of Faith, Section 56).

The subject of sanctification has caused so much misunderstanding and bitter feelings, and has been so seriously abused by some people, I that many dread to use the word. Yet the word is not only a Bible term, but it is one that has depth of meaning. No matter how much it has been abused, it is not wisdom to give up the use of the term or the acceptance. of the truth it suggests.

Sanctification is not a second work of grace that some people talk about and some profess to have. Sanctification is not the doing away with the carnal nature.

There is such a thing as the carnal nature, but it is not something material- something we can pull out as we would pull out a bad tooth. A carnal nature is a nature controlled by the will of the flesh. While it is the believer's privilege to have his mind, his nature, controlled by the Holy Spirit, even in that case, the fleshly nature is not removed, but is simply put side in preference to the spiritual control. We still have the flesh and will have it as long as we are in this world. As Christians we should live after the spirit and not after the flesh. But the flesh will remain with us.

The Confession of Faith says, "A state of sinless perfection in this life is not authorized by the Scripture and is a dogma of dangerous tendency." The reason for this statement is the fact that our fathers had actually seen what a belief in this doctrine did for people. It is dangerous because it is deceiving. It puts too much self-confidence in the minds of people and subjects them to many dangers of which they are not conscious. When sin is an open enemy, it is much easier to combat than when it is secret.

The Bible alone tells what sanctification is, and that *it is the practice of setting apart or the state of being set apart* for God. Repeatedly in the Old Testament the law describes how the priests and others were to go through the process of sanctifying things and persons, as well as themselves. In Leviticus 8: 10-12 we have one case of Moses, who took the anointing oil, and sanctified the tabernacle, then the vessels of the tabernacle and then Aaron. In another passage in Leviticus we are told that a man can sanctify his house, meaning that he can set it apart as a gift to the Lord. In another place we are told that a man can sanctify a part of his field to the Lord, meaning that he can designate a part of his land as the Lord's, and all the produce from that part of the field is to be the Lord's.

Also, the word has another meaning, according to the teachings of the Bible. *It means to cleanse, to separate from moral or ceremonial uncleanliness.* The priests were told to sanctify themselves before the performed any official duties. The people had to sanctity themselves before they could come into the presence of God.

The two meanings of the word are closely related, for one cannot be completely set apart to the service of God without being separated from sin; nor can one be separated from sin without wanting to be completely set apart for the service of God.

To be sanctified, to repeat, means to be set apart for the service of God as special vessels, separated ones, and as these special vessels we must separate ourselves from the sins of the world.

How are Men Sanctified?

Naturally, the question arises, *How* are men sanctified? In First Thessalonians 5:23, we are clearly taught that the process of sanctification is the work of God: "And the very God of peace sanctify you wholly." In Hebrews 10:10, we are taught, "We are sanctified through the offering of the body of Jesus Christ once for all." Just as the blood of the sacrificial lamb in the land of Egypt set the children of Israel apart from the people of Egypt, so the sacrifice of Jesus Christ set apart the believer in him from the unbeliever. The blood of Jesus Christ purchased the believer for God, set him apart as a special possession of God. The question concerning how the blood of Jesus sanctifies us is harder for man to understand. The only explanation that is possible, and the only one that is necessary, is that the blood of Jesus cleanses us from all guilt of sin, and thus separates us from the mass of men under the curse of the broken law.

John 17:17 says, "Sanctify them through thy truth; thy word is truth." But in what sense does the Word of God sanctify us? As we bring ourselves into daily contact with the Word of God, our lives and our hearts are disclosed, and we see their imperfections and put them away. Thus we are more separated from the sins of our lives through the truths of God's Word and are separated to God.

The Bible also teaches that we have a part in this process of sanctification. In Hebrews 12:14 we are taught to "Follow peace with all men, and holiness (sanctification) without which no man shall see the Lord." Sanctification is something to be sought for, to be followed after. While it is God's work in our lives, our part of it is to make it the object of our earnest desires and pursuit. It is our part to present our bodies a living sacrifice to God instead of making them the servants of sin.

In Acts 26: 18 we learn that sanctification, just like regeneration, is conditioned upon faith in Jesus Christ. We can claim sanctification upon simple faith in Jesus and by surrendering our lives to him.

When Are Men Sanctified?

If we accept the truth as to *how* men are sanctified, it is easy to answer the question as to *when* they are sanctified. If sanctification is the act of God that comes to men when they accept Jesus Christ through faith and turn from the sins to the life he has given them, then it takes place when the believer is born into the kingdom. It is right then that he becomes set apart for the Lord; then that he is bought with a price; then that he has his old sins rolled away and becomes a new creature in Jesus Christ; then that he is cleansed from the imperfections of his past and is united with God through Jesus Christ. The experience does not have to be repeated year after year, as did the ceremonial cleansings of the Jews; but it has been done once for all in the death of Jesus Christ, and is applied to our lives through our act of faith that leads to regeneration.

Of course, the process is not finished completely at that time, in one sense. As we grow in grace and in the knowledge of our Lord and Savior Jesus Christ, we find more ways in which we can be set apart for his service. We find more imperfections in our lives, and we seek cleansing and freedom from them. It will not be completely finished until we have been taken home to Jesus Christ, but it is a reality all along the way. This truth is borne out by Section 57 of our

Confession of Faith which says: "Growth in grace is secured by personal consecration to the service of God, regular attention to the means of grace, the reading of the Holy Scriptures, prayer, the ministrations of the sanctuary, and all known Christian duties. By such means the believer's faith is much increased, his tendency to sin weakened, the lusts of the flesh mortified, and he more and more strengthened in all saving graces, and in the practice of holiness, without which no man shall see the Lord."

Sanctification is not something to be wondered at, to be shunned; it is the possession of every true believer in Jesus Christ who has been bought by the blood of Jesus Christ, cleansed from his sins and set apart to God's service. It is accomplished by God the Father, Son and Holy Spirit and is a continual process to be completed when we gather around the throne with him. "I beseech you therefore, brethren, by the mercies of God, that ye present your bodies a living sacrifice, holy, acceptable unto God, which is your reasonable service" (Romans 12:1).

SUBJECTS FOR FURTHER STUDY

1. Sections 51-55 of the Confession of Faith on Regeneration
2. The place of repentance in regeneration, Sections 42-44 of the Confession of Faith
3. The part which the freedom of will plays in regeneration, Sections 34-37 of the Confession of Faith
4. The Scripture references under Section 56 of the Confession of Faith
5. The place of faith in regeneration, Sections 45-47 of the Confession of Faith
6. The contrast between the Christian religion and other religions in the method of justification
7. Sections 48-50 of the Confession of Faith, with the Scripture references
8. What is meant by good works? Sections 58, 59 of the Confession of Faith
9. The place of faith in the Old Testament
10. The full meaning of the term "atonement"
11. The part which growth in grace plays in sanctification
12. The difference between the doctrine of growth in grace and the doctrine of growth into grace
13. Methods of sanctification in the Old Testament

7

Preservation
of Believers

"Those whom God has justified, He will also glorify; consequently, the truly regenerated soul will not totally fall away from a state of grace, but will be preserved to everlasting life."

"The preservation of believers depends on the unchangeable love and power of God, the merits, advocacy, and intercession of Jesus Christ, the abiding of the Holy Spirit and seed of God within them, and the nature of the Covenant of Grace. Nevertheless, true believers, through the temptations of Satan, the world, and the flesh, and the neglect of the means of grace, may fall into sin, incur God's displeasure, and grieve the Holy Spirit, and thus be deprived of some measure of their graces and comforts, and have their consciences wounded; but the Christian will never rest satisfied therein.

"God continues to forgive the sins of those who are justified, and although He will never permit them to fall from the state of justification, yet they may, by their sins, fall under God's fatherly displeasure, and not have the light of His countenance restored unto them until they humble themselves, confess their sins, and renew their consecration to God" (Cumberland Presbyterian Confession of Faith, Sections 50, 60, 61).

What Is Our Position?

The Cumberland Presbyterian Church is peculiar in its doctrine, in the sense that it accepts a middle ground theology. It is not Calvinistic, and it is not Arminian in its teachings. That is, it does not believe that God has fixed the affairs of this world so that man has no choice of his own; neither does it believe that, regardless of man's actions or experiences, he cannot be sure of heaven until he dies.

Our Confession of Faith teaches that "the truly regenerated soul will not totally fall away from a state of grace, but will be preserved to everlasting life."

What Are the Grounds for Our Position?

Those who believe in this doctrine base it on the fact that when a man has been born into the kingdom of God, he becomes a child of God in a peculiar sense, and being born in this spiritual sense will not be unborn; the fact that Jesus Christ, who died for us, also lives to make intercession for us; and the fact that the Holy Spirit is in the world today to aid us in living this victorious life.

The argument as to the in-dwelling seed of Christ in the life of a regenerated person does not take away his freedom, but rather establishes him as a son of God in this new sense. He is then in a position to accept the pleadings of Jesus in his behalf, and is ready to accept the assistance of the Holy Spirit in his life. Having been born, if the term is a logical one, he will not be unborn. Just as the child may not develop as he should, and may not reach the size he should, so the regenerated man may not grow in grace as he should; but he does not therefore cease to be a child of God.

However, it is especially the intercession of Christ and the help of the Holy Spirit that we wish to consider. There are a number of passages of scripture which teach the strengthening truth of the intercession of Christ. For instance, Romans 8:34 says, "It is Christ that died, yea rather, that is risen again, who is even at the right hand of God, who also maketh intercession for us. Who shall separate us from the love of Christ? Shall tribulation, or distress, or persecution, or famine, or nakedness, or peril, or sword?" "My little children, these things write I unto you, that ye sin not. And if any man sin, we have an advocate with the Father, Jesus Christ the Righteous: and he is the propitiation for our sins: and not for ours, only, but also for the sins of the whole world" (I John 2: 1, 2) is a passage that plainly states that, if anyone of these little children to whom John is writing sins, he has a counsel to represent him at the throne of God.

Hebrews 7:25 states that Jesus is "able to save them to the uttermost that come unto God by him, seeing he ever liveth to make intercession for them." The reason assigned for the fact that Jesus is able to save utterly all people is the fact that he ever liveth to make intercession for them.

John 17:9, 11, 15, 20, 21, show the attitude of Jesus toward His believing children. He prayed to God while he was in the world that God would keep his believers from evil. What may we imagine goes on continually at the throne of God now?

While the basis of the doctrine is the indwelling of Christ and his advocacy, the practical results will come from the working of the Holy Spirit. *The purpose*

of the Holy Spirit in the world is to guide us into all truth, to strengthen us for
the battles of life, to pray for us, and to produce in our lives the fruit of love.

These, in brief, are the three facts upon which the doctrine of the
preservation of believers is based. I am a believer in Jesus Christ, born into the
kingdom through faith in Him, but I am weak, and may be led astray at any
time; but, "if any man sin, we have an advocate with the Father." Still, I might
despair if I did not have the assurance that the Holy Spirit would help me in
times of my weakness. Jesus said, "I will not leave you comfortless; I will send
you another comforter." This comforter is to be a help to us in our lives, as
Jesus was a help to those with whom He lived while on earth.

Will the Regenerated Fall?

The most prevalent question asked when this doctrine is being discussed is,
"Will the truly regenerated soul fall from grace?" The truth of the scripture is
the best answer to any argument, and we have this answer in John 10:27-29:
"My sheep hear my voice, and I know them, and they follow me: and I give
unto them eternal life; and they shall never perish, neither shall any man pluck
them out of my hand. My Father, which gave them to me, is greater than all;
and no man is able to pluck them out of my Father's hand." To make the
expression more emphatic, the original really means, "They shall by no means
ever destroy themselves, neither shall any man pluck them out of my hand."

There is a similar thought in Romans 8:35-39: "Who shall separate us from
the love of Christ? Shall tribulation, or distress, or persecution, or famine, or
nakedness, or peril, or sword? . . . Nay, in all these things we are more than
conquerors through him that loved us. For I am persuaded that neither death nor
life, nor angels, nor principalities, nor powers, nor things present, nor things to
come, nor height, nor depth, nor any other creature shall be able to separate us
from the love of God, which is in Christ Jesus our Lord."

Other passages along this same line are Philippians 1:6, Psalm 94:14, First
Corinthians 1:8, and Psalm 34:7.

Some words of Jesus regarding the eternal nature of the Christian should
be sufficient to satisfy us: "Verily, verily, I say unto you, he that heareth my
word, and believeth on him that sent me, hath everlasting life, and shall not
come into condemnation, but is passed from death unto life" (John 5:24). "Thou
art Peter, and upon this rock I will build my church; and the gates of hell shall
not prevail against it" (Matthew 16:18). His description of the victorious life
was that of a man who built his house on the rock.

What of Objections?

However, a discussion of this subject would not be complete unless the
objections to the doctrine were reviewed.

The passage in Ezekiel 18:20 which is so often quoted against the doctrine:

"The soul that sinneth, it shall die," can be explained by referring the reader to the context which makes it clear that the prophet is trying to place the guilt of sin on the individual instead of upon his descendants or relatives. But, even if one maintains that the passage should be interpreted in another way, "If a man sin, we have an advocate."

The parable of the sower who scattered the seed can be explained by showing that Jesus clearly states the reason for the plants growing up and withering away as being the fact that they had no depth of soil. They were not deep enough to get the substance. There are many cases of people who seem to spring up suddenly in the Christian religion and then to go out as quickly. These people are like the plants in this story. Because their lives were not rooted and grounded in Christ, they had no depth of soil. But it will be noted from the story, also, that there were plants which had depth of soil and brought forth an abundant harvest. They were like the truly regenerated soul.

The statement of Paul in First Timothy 1: 18-20 about some making shipwreck concerning the faith, clearly refers to the teaching of the doctrine and not to the individual's practice of faith in his life.

In Hebrews 10:26-29 we have a hypothetical case presented which has been used by those who believe in falling from grace. The case says, "If we sin wilfully after that we have received the knowledge of the truth, there remaineth no more sacrifice for sins. . . He that despised Moses' law died without mercy under two or three witnesses: Of how much sorer punishment, suppose ye, shall he be thought worthy who has trodden under foot the Son of God, and hath counted the blood of the covenant, wherewith he was sanctified, an unholy thing, and hath done despite unto the Spirit of grace?" This imaginary case does not state that the person has been regenerated, but that he has received the knowledge of truth. We have many examples of men who have had a knowledge of the truth without accepting it. The sense in which he has been sanctified by the blood of the covenant is that he was ransomed by the blood of Jesus; but he did not accept the blood. He might have entered, but he despised the privilege, and died in his sins.

Sometimes the argument for apostasy takes the form of the parable of the man who drove out the unclean spirit (Matthew 12:43-45). But he simply cleaned house. He placed nothing there in place of the unclean spirit. He did not have the indwelling spirit of Christ.

One of the most difficult passages to explain is Hebrews 6:4.6, which declares, "It is impossible for those who were once enlightened, and have tasted of the heavenly gift, and were made partakers of the Holy Ghost, and have tasted the good word of God, and the powers of the world to come, if they shall fall away, to renew them again unto repentance; seeing they crucify to themselves the Son of God afresh, and put him to an open shame."

If this means to teach that apostasy is possible after regeneration, it teaches more than is ordinarily taught by those who hold this doctrine. It teaches, in that case, that, if one ever falls from that state of grace, it is impossible to renew him. Such is not the belief of those who hold the doctrine of apostasy, for we have hundreds of cases of those who say that they have fallen from grace, but who come back and live godly lives afterward.

Notice what is really said about this person in the scriptures. He had been taught the principles and doctrines of Christianity, had enjoyed the privileges of the new religion, had experienced various gifts, had cherished the hopes of the gospel; but it does not say that he had experienced the new birth. He could have done all these things and never have experienced the act of regeneration. His apostasy, then, was simply turning from the true religion which had been presented to him to another religion such as Judaism or heathenism. These people to whom the passage is addressed had been on the edge of Christianity without having come into it; therefore, they had apostatized from the Christian religion, but not from a state of grace.

The Scriptures are clear in their statements in favor of our doctrine. The objections are based on hypothesis. Which should we accept?

But What Does the Bible Teach?

In order to be perfectly fair, we should examine the cases that are recorded in the Bible, and which seem to teach falling from grace.

What should be said about the example of David, who started out so well, but who committed a great sin? The only thing that can be said is that David sinned; but he had an Advocate with the Father, and he came back to a glorious end as the "Sweet Singer of Israel," who gave us some of the great psalms for our worship.

Solomon started out well, also, and sinned grievously. But he had an Advocate with the Father; and, if the writings of the Bible which are attributed to him are authentic, he came back to a glorious end. If those writings are not his, then we can say that certainly the people who lived immediately after Solomon, or at least years before our day, believed that Solomon was the kind of character who would have written such books as Ecclesiastes, Proverbs, and the Songs of Solomon.

What should be said about Judas, who betrayed Jesus? The big question here is: If Judas were a bad man, why was he selected as a disciple by Jesus? I do not know. Maybe it was to show us that we are not to expect a perfect church in the world. But, regardless of why it was done, Jesus plainly said some time before the betrayal that he had chosen the twelve and that one of them was a devil. Judas is never represented as a good man. He is always mentioned last in the list of disciples. Every indication toward him is that he was bad from the beginning. Jesus certainly must not be accused of making a mistake, of being fooled in his choice of what he thought was a good man.

Finally, Peter started out well, and then denied his Lord; but Jesus looked at him with an expression that melted the heart of the great disciple. He had been told before that Satan had desired him to sift him like wheat, but that Jesus had prayed for him. He had an Advocate that enabled him to become the leader of the early Christian Church among the Jews.

It seems that these outstanding cases of men who started out well and then committed sin are sufficient evidence to show that the fact that a man sins is not evidence that he has fallen from grace, and the fact that God's Spirit is still over the lives of his children.

What About Personal Experience?

What shall we say about cases we know of in our own personal experience-people who have started out well, and then turned to a life of indifference or of open sin? *There are two possible solutions that* we *shall examine briefly.*

First, they were never Christians, but simply mistaken in their own hearts or trying to fool others. There are such, according to Matthew 7:22, 23: "Many will say to me in that day, Lord, Lord, have we not prophesied in thy name? And in thy name have cast out devils? And in thy name done many wonderful works? And then will I profess unto them, I never knew you; depart from me, ye that work iniquity."

Second, they may have had the foundation of Jesus Christ, but built upon it with cheap materials. "If any man build upon this foundation gold, silver, precious stones, wood, hay, stubble; every man's work shall be made manifest: for the day shall declare it, because it shall be revealed by fire; and the fire shall try every man's work of what sort it is. If any man's work abide which he hath built thereupon, he shall receive a reward. If any man's work shall be burned, he shall suffer loss; but he himself shall be saved; yet so as by fire" (I Corinthians 3:12-15). Certainly, no truth could be plainer than this passage.

With regard to these cases from personal experience, it is sufficient to say that the Bible is the standard, and not the appearance or seeming experience of man. How can we tell what is true on the inside of man?

What May We Conclude?

Our salvation is not dependent upon what we *do or say, but upon the shed blood of Jesus Christ.* "Believe on the Lord Jesus Christ and thou shalt be saved." "He that believeth on him is not condemned," but is "kept by the power of God through faith unto salvation."

Jesus Christ plainly taught, and the Bible teaches about him, that it was his great love which caused him to die for the salvation of the people. No one denies that truth, nor does anyone deny that Christ is able to save those who come to him. Then may we ask ourselves the question: Is it possible that Christ could love a soul enough to save it and, then say to that soul, "Now since you have salvation, let me see if YOU can keep it"? Does it take greater power to keep a soul than it does to save it?

The truly regenerated man will always choose to keep his religion. If he should lose it, it would be against his will. He desires to continue in a saved state until his nature is changed, and we believe that nothing but the power of God can change human nature.

Man accepts salvation with the idea that it is an everlasting covenant (Jeremiah 32:40). God's design is changed if eternal life is lost. Crisman refers to an imaginary scene in heaven which describes what would be true if a saved soul could be lost. He says that upon an announcement of this fact the young angels begin to rejoice and praise God with loud Hosannas, but the more experienced command silence and say, "Rejoice not yet, lest your joy be premature." "Methinks all rejoicing would cease in the celestial abode and gloomy suspense reign supreme until human events were wound to a close and it was decided which of God's children were saved and which were lost," Crisman declares.

Hebrews 12:2 says that we are "looking unto Jesus the author and finisher of our faith." If he be the finisher, as he is the author, there can be no failure.

Does this doctrine lead to immorality? A good way to judge would be simply to compare the lives of Presbyterians and Baptists, who agree more or less on this doctrine, with the lives of Methodists and Christians, who disagree. If it can be shown that there is more immorality or lack of piety in the first group than in the second because of this teaching, then it should be ruled out as a doctrine. But since the Bible teaches it, and such cannot be shown, the doubtful experiences of a few persons should not destroy our faith in a precious doctrine.

Sometimes people will say, "If I should believe a doctrine like that, I would do anything I wanted to and still believe that I would be saved." But such a statement is not logical and shows a gross misunderstanding of the nature and the purpose of the doctrine. If anyone should take advantage of this doctrine to do things which he knows are not in keeping with the Christian principles, that within itself would be certain evidence that he is not a truly regenerated soul. Is there anything in this doctrine which would inspire a person to live carelessly or to live beneath the privileges of a Christian? The doctrine is based on the indwelling of Christ in the life. Is there anything about that fact which would make a person want to live carelessly? It is based on a knowledge of the teachings that Christ is constantly praying that every Christian will be able to live a victorious Christian life. Is there anything in that fact which would make a person want to live carelessly? It is also based on the fact that the Holy Spirit is continually working with the Christian to get him to live as Christ lived. Is there anything in that teaching which would make a person want to live carelessly?

The best guarantee a person can have that he will live a good life is as follows: 1) Good heritage, or the kind of birth which will give him a good start in life. 2) The knowledge that somebody cares for him and is deeply concerned that he live up to the highest possible standards. 3) The wise counsel of one who knows the dangers and who knows how to avoid them. Any child who has such a guarantee as this will not be very prone to go wrong and will certainly not take advantage of the fact to do as he pleases.

It is just such a guarantee of Christian success that the doctrine of the preservation of believers offers. Instead of being something to take advantage of to live a cheap life, the doctrine undoubtedly inspires to live a Christian life.

THOUGHTS FOR FURTHER STUDY
1. The Confession of Faith, Sections 60-65
2. The meaning of Christian assurance, and its practical benefits
3. Could any other term describe regeneration better than the one which Jesus used: "The New Birth"?
4. What effect does this term have upon the doctrine of preservation?
5. The extremes to which pure Calvinism and pure Arminianism go
6. Meaning of "those whom God has justified, he will also glorify"

8

Baptism

"Water baptism is . . . a sign or symbol of the baptism of the Holy Spirit. Baptism is rightly administered by pouring or sprinkling water upon the person, yet the validity of this sacrament does not depend upon any particular mode of administration" (Cumberland Presbyterian Confession of Faith, extracts from Sections 105 and 107).

How Liberal Are We?

In this, as in all other parts of its work and worship, the Cumberland Presbyterian Church is liberal enough to allow any man the right to his own opinion. It has an opinion of its own, which it is able to back up with sufficient scriptural proof, and then states that it will allow the other man to interpret the Scriptures as he sees fit, and will even accept that man with his interpretation if he desires to unite with the Cumberland Presbyterian Church. Some people think they have grounds for believing that water baptism should be administered by immersing the person in water, or the doctrine never would have lived as long as it has and attracted the persons it has. On the other hand, there are grounds for the belief that it is rightly administered by sprinkling or pouring, or three-fourths (some say nine-tenths) of the Christian world would not administer it in that way.

We have no quarrel with those who wish to interpret the Scriptures in their own way, but we maintain that *they have no right to say that their way is the only way* to interpret them. We have no quarrel with those who interpret baptism as a sacrament to be administered by immersion, but we say that they have no right to teach that those who have been sprinkled have not been baptized.

68

Some will be tempted to say in the beginning that since water baptism is a mere outward ceremony, it is not worth disputing about. At that point we agree, since no doctrine should cause a dispute between believers. But, if it were worthwhile for Jesus to approve such an ordinance, it is worthwhile for us to try to find out what he meant by it. And, so long as some of the largest denominations of Protestantism are divided on that point primarily, it is worthwhile to try to find some method of removing the difficulty.

Some people think that to have a mode of baptism is narrow and that we ought to allow people to be baptized in any way that they want just to satisfy them. Such is not a sensible view. To accept a certain mode is not more unreasonable than it is to accept a certain form of government, open communion as opposed to closed communion, and the: preservation of believers as opposed to falling from grace. Our view is not narrow, but is scriptural and sensible.

What Is Our View?

The Cumberland Presbyterian Church believes that water baptism is "a sign or symbol of the baptism of the Holy Spirit" and "is rightly administered by pouring or sprinkling water upon the person.""This seems clear enough to those who know the way the Holy Spirit was always represented as coming upon persons in the Bible record. In the Confession of Faith there is no justification for any other mode of baptism whatever. We do not teach that baptism is a symbol of the death, burial, and resurrection of Jesus, and for that reason we do not practice baptism by immersion. *We say that it is a sign of one thing, and that that one thing is the baptism of the Holy Spirit.* A sign or a symbol must represent the thing for which it stands, and two divergent things cannot be represented by the same sign, nor can two divergent signs represent the same thing. To practice both forms of baptism is to destroy all of its symbolism and make it mean nothing as a sign.

Some people expect Cumberland Presbyterians to practice either form of baptism, as the subject may desire. But such a request is absurd. Would you ask a Baptist minister to baptize you by sprinkling? Would you ask an Episcopal minister to immerse you? You certainly would not, because you know that their symbol represents a certain thing to them. For that same reason it is absurd to ask a Cumberland Presbyterian to use both forms. We have but one form, and that is set forth in Sections 99 and 103 of the Confession of Faith and Section 16 of the Directory of Worship.

It is true that some people interpret Section 101 of the Confession of Faith as a justification for the use of either of the modes of baptism. But those who know when and why that section was placed in the Confession will tell you that it gives no justification for the practice of immersion. It is in our Confession to show that *when a person comes from another church with a letter, we will not require that person to be baptized by our mode.* We simply accept his baptism, as we do his letter, as a valid baptism regardless of its mode.

The General Assembly in 1960 had presented to it a question from New Hope Presbytery as follows: "Is it legal according to the Confession of Faith for a Cumberland Presbyterian minister to administer the sacrament of baptism through the form of immersion?" After noting that our Confession of Faith says that water baptism has but one meaning and that is as the sign or symbol of the baptism of the Holy Spirit and that it has but one statement regarding how it should be done (through pouring or sprinkling water upon the person), the Assembly overwhelmingly adopted the following statement: "We therefore answer the question in the memorial from New Hope Presbytery by saying that the baptism of a person who has been immersed is not illegal, but that immersion as a form of baptism is out of keeping with the doctrine to which Cumberland Presbyterian ministers have subscribed and is without meaning according to our interpretation as to what water baptism signifies. Ministers who have stated that they sincerely adopt the meaning which is clearly set forth in our Confession of Faith should guide their conduct accordingly." In doing this, our General Assembly clearly ruled that we have but one form of baptism, although we will accept the baptism of any other recognized church when a member transfers to our denomination.

What Is Its Scriptural Basis?

Let us see upon what Scriptural basis this position is founded.

In the Great Commission as recorded in Matthew 28:19, 20, Jesus told his disciples, and us, "Go ye, therefore, and teach all nations, baptizing them in the name of the Father, and the Son, and of the Holy Ghost; teaching them to observe all things whatsoever I have commanded you." If this word "baptize" was understood by Jesus to mean immerse, then baptism should not be done by sprinkling or pouring; if he meant to sprinkle, then it should not be done by immersion. If he meant by it to convey the idea of ceremonial cleansing or purification by water, then it should be done according to the method of the ceremonial cleansing.

There are four words in the command: "Go," "disciple," "baptize," "teach." When Jesus told them to go, he did not say how. If he had said for them to walk, they would have done wrong to run, or to ride. When he said, "make disciples of," he did not say they must win all of them in a certain way. He did not win his disciples in one definite way, and we do not do so today. When he said "teach," he did not limit that to a particular method. In other words, the terms are general. Is it reasonable to suppose that Jesus would have used three general terms and then would have inserted a word which was particular without calling some attention to that particular word? Certainly, Jesus did not refer to mode here, but to the idea of ceremonial purification by water.

We are commanded to go into all the world with the gospel, but we are not commanded to go in the same way the disciples did. We are told to preach, but we are not told to sit down as we preach, as they did. We are told to observe the Lord's Supper, but we are not told to eat it while reclining at a table. They went about doing good, wearing loose flowing robes and open sandals, but we are not commanded to dress in that way while we go about doing good. We are told to baptize in the name of the Father, the Son and the Holy Ghost, but the method is not conveyed in the message. That is not conceding the rightness of the belief that the disciples baptized by immersion, as we shall see later. The fact that we are trying to establish is that the Great Commission does not prescribe a method, but a general ceremonial purification.

And even if every Old Testament and New Testament case could be proven to be immersion, would we be compelled to follow that practice today? Do we do everything else just as they did? We have learned to adapt our practices to the needs and conditions of men.

To strengthen the idea that baptism means purification, we may examine the words of John the Baptist, "I, indeed, baptize you with water, but one mightier than I cometh, the latchet of whose shoes I am not worthy to unloose: He shall baptize you with the Holy Ghost and with fire" (Luke 3:16). Understanding the word "baptize" to mean purification or cleansing, the meaning is clear. John's cleansing was by water; Christ's should be by the Spirit and by fire, an evident advance in thought which is entirely natural, and with the thought of purification running through the whole. And to make it even plainer, the very next clause reads: "whose fan is in his hand, and he will thoroughly purge his floor, and will gather the wheat into his garner; but the chaff he will burn with fire unquenchable" (Luke 3:17).

John the Baptist should be called John the Purifier. He was a stern, rigid, uncompromising man. The people came to him confessing their sins. He preached to them in plain truths, pointing to One who would be revealed, One who would thoroughly purify them. They would naturally think of the prophecy of four hundred years before: "Behold, I will send my messenger, and he shall prepare the way before me: and the Lord, whom ye seek, shall suddenly come to his temple, even the messenger of the covenant, whom ye delight in: behold, he shall come, saith the Lord of Hosts. But who may abide the day of his coming? and who shall stand when he appeareth? For he is like a refiner's fire, and like fullers' rope: and he shall sit as a refiner and purifier of silver; and he shall purify the sons of Levi, and purge them as gold and silver, that they may offer unto the Lord an offering in righteousness" (Malachi 3:1-3).

The prophecy referred to the coming of the Christ, and his forerunner, and they were looking for a purifier. With that in mind, you can understand the question of the priests as they came to John and said, "Why baptizeth thou, then, if thou be not that Christ, nor Elias, neither that prophet?" (John 1:25).

They were looking for the coming of the Christ who would fulfill the prophecy concerning a purifier, and they called it baptism.

Another passage will show the same meaning. When Jesus and his disciples came to the territory where John was baptizing, there "arose a question between some of John's disciples and the Jews about purifying" (John 3:25), and the disciples went to John about the question of Jesus' baptizing the people. The whole matter shows the close connection between the terms "baptism" and "purification."

What of Purification?

The next question is: How does that purification take place according to the Old Testament teachings?

In one of the Apocryphal books (Ecclesiasticus 34:25) we read, "He that is purified (baptizomenos) from a dead body, and touches it again, what does his cleansing profit him?" We may assume that the writer understood the process of this purification as it was laid down in the nineteenth chapter of Numbers, where it is required that the ashes of a heifer should be put into a vessel, running water should be put thereto, and this water should be sprinkled upon the man with a bunch of hyssop in the hand of a clean person. Nothing more was required. Therefore, the man that had touched a dead body and was not thus purified should be cut off from his people, because "the water of separation was not sprinkled upon him" (Numbers 19:13).

It is this practice that is referred to in Hebrews 9:13, 14: "For if .... the ashes of an heifer, sprinkling the unclean, sanctifieth to the purifying of the flesh, how much more shall the blood of Christ. . . purge your conscience from dead works to serve the living God?" And in like manner in the next chapter (10:22) he speaks of having "our hearts sprinkled from an evil conscience."

The entire process of cleansing from a dead body was by sprinkling, and two hundred years earlier it was called baptism by the writer of Ecclesiasticus, Jesus the Son of Sirach. Josephus who wrote about two hundred and fifty years later (in 93 or 94 A.D.), and who is still looked upon as one of the greatest Jewish historians, understood the Jewish customs, and he called this sprinkling "baptism." He says, "Baptizing by this ashes put into the spring water, they sprinkled on the third and seventh days" *(Antiquities,* Book 4, Chapter 4). These two quotations show that the word had been used for two or three hundred years to mean purification by sprinkling. If Jesus had intended to convey any other meaning, it seems that he would have stated it.

Another Jewish custom in the time of Jesus is recorded in Mark 7: 2-4: "And when they saw some of His disciples eat bread with defiled, that is to say with unwashen hands, they found fault, for the Pharisees, and all the Jews, except they wash their hands (with the fist) eat not, holding the tradition of the elders. And when they come from the market, except they wash (baptize themselves), they eat not. And many other things there be which they have received to hold, as the washing (baptizing) of cups and pots, brazen vessels, and of tables." In the East many persons go to the market several times a day. Immersion would be an impractical burden after each trip to the market. Furthermore, Mark makes it a ceremonial cleansing altogether. At the market someone might come into contact with an unclean person, a leper, or someone *who* had touched a dead body. He needed to be cleansed to care for this possibility. He had no law except to do it by sprinkling after a certain fashion.

In addition, as this verse says, it had to be done in running water. All the laws plainly stated that it must be "living water," that is, running water. When one entered a house in that country a servant met him at the door and poured water over the hands. The guests would not think of dipping the hands in "dead" water. The water pouring over the hands made it "running water."

In case a person had no attendant to pour this water for him, he took the pitcher in one hand and poured the water over the other hand. Then he changed hands and went through the process again. If there were no pitcher, he baptized his hands "with the fist", that is, by dipping the water with one fist and then with the other and pouring it from his hand over the other hand.

In Luke 11: 38 we have the record of the visit of Jesus to the house of a Pharisee, "And when the Pharisee saw it, he marveled that he had not first washed (baptized) before dinner." It is hard to believe that Jesus was expected to be immersed before he ate his dinner. He had been out in the multitude, and the Pharisee thought Jesus should go through the ceremonial cleansing, as recorded in Mark 7, before he ate his dinner.

The account of the miracle of Jesus at the feast of Cana of Galilee is interesting and enlightening. They ran out of wine for the feast, and the mother of Jesus called him to help the host. He told the servant to fill the water pots with water. Why were all of these pots there? "There were set six water pots of stone after the manner of the purifying of the Jews." From the pots the guests had taken water, or the servants had done it for them, and had sprinkled themselves for the customary ceremonial cleansing before the feast (John 2:6). Not even the hands of the guests were in these pots. The pots were so clean that Jesus did not even tell the servants to cleanse them before they filled them with the water that he turned into wine.

These seem to be sufficient evidences that purifying, which was spoken of as baptism, was performed by pouring water over the hands or the body, and not by immersing in a basin or pool.

In these cases, we have a picture of how ceremonial purification was accomplished. And we have seen that it was a symbol of spiritual cleansing. Can we not also see that our spiritual purification is symbolized by baptism? Our spiritual cleansing comes through the work of the Holy Spirit in our lives and by that only. The death, burial and resurrection of Jesus are of no avail to us until we have made a personal acceptance of them through the work of the Holy Spirit in us. But when the Holy Spirit cleanses us, we are spiritually clean. And it is this great fact in the spiritual life which we represent by our baptism.

What Do the Biblical Records of Baptism Indicate?

Let us examine some of the Biblical records regarding baptism.

When Jesus was talking to Nicodemus, he made the statement that a man must be born again. Nicodemus did not understand him. Jesus had used figurative language, and Nicodemus knew it. Therefore, he said, in substance, "I know you do not mean that a man must be born again in a physical way, but what do you mean? " Then Jesus replied, "Except a man be born of water and of the Spirit, he cannot enter into the kingdom of God" (John 3:5).

What Jesus is referring to here is simply the natural birth and the spiritual birth. Being "born of water" was without doubt a well-known form of speech which Christ used to refer to natural birth, as will be testified to by any doctor of medicine. Without this interpretation, it is impossible to harmonize the answer of Jesus with the question asked him. He further states in support of this interpretation that "that which is born of the flesh is flesh; and that which is born of the spirit is spirit." "Born of the water" in the first expression and "born of the flesh" in the second are equivalent terms.

If you make "born of the water" refer to water baptism, you must I have three births instead of the two to which Jesus referred: you must be born of the flesh, born of the water, and born of the Spirit. Then Jesus should have said, "Ye must be born twice more"; for Nicodemus had been born but by the flesh. Furthermore, why did Jesus put water baptism first, if this means water baptism? Was that Jesus' way of doing things? Did he ordinarily mention the ceremony before the thing signified? No, He always put the reality first, and then put all lesser things after that.

Some people get a great deal of support for immersion from the passage in the sixth chapter of Romans, which refers to being buried with Christ in baptism. All the argument that is necessary to destroy its force for immersion is to examine the context. That connection undertakes to show the utter inconsistency of a Christian profession with a continued life in sin. The whole argument of the apostle is upon the meaning of baptism instead of upon the mode.

Possibly a brief reference should be made to the cases of baptism in the New Testament. In the case of Philip and the eunuch (Acts 8), we find that the eunuch was riding along in his chariot and reading in the neighborhood of Isaiah 53. Philip asked him if he understood what he was reading; and, upon being told that he did not, Philip began to preach Jesus unto him. It is natural to suppose that Philip would not begin simply where the eunuch was reading to explain the life and work of Jesus, but would go back to the beginning of the thought. If that be true, it is easy to see that he could turn to the close of the fifty-second chapter of the same book from which the eunuch was reading and read the passage, "So shall he sprinkle many nations;" and when they read that and the eunuch saw some water, he said, "Why should not I be baptized?" (52:15). The thing that probably suggested the baptism to him was the statement that this Jesus about whom Philip was preaching was said to sprinkle many nations.

When Paul was baptized, Ananias came into the room: and after an introduction of his purposes, he told Paul to ARISE and be baptized.

When Peter preached at Caesarea and the Holy Spirit fell on all the people who heard the word, Peter said, "Can any man forbid water, that these should not be baptized, as well as we?" Forbidding the water sounds as though the water was to be brought instead of taking. the people to the place of the water.

The Philippian jailor was baptized at night immediately following, we suppose, his conversion in the jail.

What Then?

Let us summarize the argument for this mode of baptism as follows: Baptism is a ceremonial purification. The spiritual purification, of which baptism is a symbol, is effected by the Holy Spirit. The Spirit is universally represented as being poured out. Unless baptism is the symbol of the outpouring of the Holy Spirit, the most important event in the history of Christian experience-the event in which personal religion has its vital birth-is without a symbol. This would seem strange, since the spiritual growth is symbolized by the sacrament of the church. Why should spiritual growth be symbolized and spiritual birth be neglected? All the laws of purification in the Old Testament were carried out by means of sprinkling. Sprinkling is mentioned as a prophecy in connection with the order of things under the reign of the Messiah. Sprinkling or pouring is a mode of baptism which every disciple may observe and every pastor perform in any clime, regardless of the strength or health of any person concerned.

There are several reasons why immersion fails to symbolize death, burial and resurrection of Jesus. He died on the cross after very cruel treatment. Nothing about the mode of baptism pictures the death. In the second place, he was buried in a cave in the side of a hill, and doubtless carried into that cave and placed very tenderly in a prostrate position on a stone bed. For the mode to be symbolic of this, it is necessary for him to have been lowered in a grave in the ground such as we know. This was not the practice of his time and could not have been symbolized by lowering persons in a watery grave. In the third place, the disciples did not believe that Jesus had arisen from the dead, or that he would arise from the dead. Since they did baptize people before his death, and since they could not understand that he was to die and arise from the dead, how could their form of baptism have any meaning if it were immersion?

As a little bread may represent to us the strength which Christ alone can impart, and a little grape juice may typify his blood shed for us, so may a little water in its purity symbolize to us the cleansing power of God's spirit and grace.

Should Cumberland Presbyterian Ministers Immerse People?

This question was asked of the General Assembly in 1960, and the following answer was adopted by our highest Court:

The question asked in this memorial is, "Is it legal according to the *Confession of Faith* for a Cumberland Presbyterian minister to administer the sacrament of baptism through the form of immersion?

We would call attention to the fact that this question does not deal with the legality or validity of baptism by immersion, but it deals only with the right of a Cumberland Presbyterian minister to administer baptism through immersion.

The ordination vows taken by all of our ministers say (Question II, page 113 of the *Constitution of the Cumberland Presbyterian Church*), "Do you sincerely receive and adopt the *Confession of Faith* and the Catechism of the Cumberland Church as containing the system of doctrines taught in the Holy Scriptures?" To which it is assumed that all ordained ministers have answered in the affirmative.

The only statement of our *Confession* as to the meaning of baptism (paragraph 105) is that water baptism is "a sign or symbol of the baptism of the Holy Spirit," and "a seal of the Covenant of Grace." A sign or symbol to be of any significance must have resemblance to the thing signified. It is for this reason that we adopt the mode of baptism which we do. Our *Confession* allows for no other meaning or significance to this sacrament. All references to the Holy Spirit in a symbolic manner have to do with the outpouring of the Spirit.

The only statement as to the manner of administering baptism is that "Baptism is rightly administered by pouring or sprinkling water upon the person" (paragraph 107a). Section 16 of the *Directory of Worship* shows exactly how this is to be done.

The next part of paragraph 107 to the effect that "the validity of this sacrament does not depend upon any particular mode of administration," does not say that Cumberland Presbyterians can administer baptism in any way they see fit. What it does say is that the baptism of some person who comes to us from a denomination which practices immersion will be accepted as a valid baptism, and that the person will not be required to be baptized again, because we recognize other denominations as a part of the Church.

This is not a narrow stand. To accept a certain form of baptism is no more narrow than to accept a certain form of government. To practice only one mode of baptism is justified because we believe that it has but one significance. It signifies the outpouring of the Holy Spirit. To symbolize that, we must hold to the picture which reminds people of the outpouring of the Spirit. Nowhere in the Scriptures is the Holy Spirit shown as a pool into which people are dipped.

We therefore answer the question in the memorial from New Hope Presbytery by saying that the baptism of a person who has been immersed is not illegal, but that immersion as a form of baptism is out of keeping with the doctrine to which Cumberland Presbyterian ministers have subscribed and is without meaning according to our interpretation as to what water baptism signifies. Ministers who have stated that they sincerely adopt the meaning which is clearly set forth in our *Confession of Faith* should guide their conduct accordingly.

THOUGHTS FOR FURTHER DISCUSSION

1. The Confession of Faith, Sections 98-103
2. Beard's lectures on the subject of baptism
3. Other references in the Scriptures to ceremonial cleansings
4. The true significance of baptism
5. The place occupied by baptism in various denominations
6. Other arguments in favor of sprinkling

9

Infant Baptism

"The proper subjects of water baptism are believing adults; also infants, one or both of whose parents or guardians are believers. There is no saving efficacy in water baptism, yet it is a duty of all believers to confess Christ in this solemn ordinance, and it is also the duty of all believing parents to consecrate their children to God in baptism" (Cumberland Presbyterian Confession of Faith, Sections 102, 103).

The Cumberland Presbyterian Church has a great deal to say about the importance of infant baptism. Section 3 of the Constitution of the Church says, "The infant children of believers are, through the covenant and by right of birth, entitled to baptism, to pastoral oversight, to instruction and to the care of the Church, with a view to their embracing Christ, and thus possessing personally all the benefits of the covenant." In Section 27 of the Constitution elders are charged with the duty of urging upon parents the importance of presenting their children for baptism. In the same section they are urged always to include the names of the baptized children when granting letters to parents.

Section 16 of the Directory of Worship gives the details of the administering of this rite as follows:

"When a child is to be baptized, it should be presented before the minister by one or both of the parents.

Before baptism, let the minister use some words of instruction respecting the institution, nature, use and ends of this ordinance, showing:

That it is instituted by Christ; that it is a seal of the righteousness of faith; that the children of the faithful have no less a right to the ordinance of the gospel than the children of Abraham to circumcision under the Old Testament; that Christ commanded all nations to be baptized; that He blessed little children, declaring that of such is the kingdom of heaven; that we are, by nature, polluted, and have need of cleansing by the blood of Christ, and by the sanctifying influences of the Holy Spirit.

The minister is also to exhort the parents to the careful performance of their duty, requiring:

That they teach the child to read the Word of God; that they instruct it in the principles of our holy religion, as contained in the Scriptures of the Old and the New Testament, an excellent summary of which we have in the Confession of Faith of this Church, and in the Catechism, which are to be recommended to them as adopted by the Church for their direction and assistance in the discharge of this important duty; that they pray with and for it; that they set an example of piety and godliness before it; and endeavor, by all the means of God's appointment, to bring up their child in the nurture and admonition of the Lord.

Then the minister is to pray for a blessing to attend this ordinance; after which, calling the child by its name, he shall say:

I baptize thee in the name of the Father, and of the Son, and of the Holy Spirit.

As he pronounces these words, he is to baptize the child with water, by pouring or sprinkling it on the face of the child, without adding any other ceremony, and the whole shall be concluded with prayer."

From these statements it should be perfectly clear as to what the Cumberland Presbyterian Church thinks about infant baptism, and why and how it should be administered. The specific manner in which the minister is instructed to administer the rite should be a help also to those who sometimes wonder if the denomination does not practice both modes of baptism on adults. Since there are no other instructions regarding the ordinance for adults, it seems that this might be taken as a sample to be followed in both ceremonies.

What Is the Basis for This Doctrine?

The significance and purpose of this ordinance are in perfect keeping with the whole plan of salvation as taught by evangelical churches. Here is an ordinance which seeks to make the personal acceptance of Christ a more certain and more natural fact. The believing parents of a small child come to the altar and pledge themselves to God and to the church that they will pray with and for the child and will do all within their power to see that the child will come into a knowledge of Christ. Beginning at an early time in the life of the one which has been entrusted to them, they prepare the soil for the reception of the spiritual seed which will bring eternal life. And as the rite of baptism is administered it becomes not only a pledge on the part of the parents, but it becomes a prophecy that their prayers will not be unanswered. It seems to say that they are so sure that their prayers and training will bring results that they can, by this act of faith, look forward through the years and see its fulfillment. In the memory of the child as it grows up, this ceremony becomes a powerful suggestion to do what the parents pledged to bring to pass.

That infants or minors were in the Old Testament community of faith is beyond question (see Genesis 17). Their being there was by the authority of God and not something which man invented. They were entitled to the rights and privileges of the faithful. Under the more humane and loving institution of the Christian Church, can anyone give them less than they enjoyed under the older order?

"But," someone objects, "Old Testament religion was quite different from that in the New Testament."

The outward forms of service are changed, but the leading moral and spiritual principles involved are the same. The religion of the Old and New Testaments is identical so far as it relates to the nature of the believer's covenant with God and the foundation of his hopes for heaven. The faith of the Christian is the faith of Abraham and the prophets of old. The covenant which the Christian enters into with his God is the same as the Abrahamic covenant, as far as its spiritual import is concerned. Romans 4: 11, 16 supports this point: "And he received the sign of circumcision, a seal of righteousness of the faith which he had yet being uncircumcised: that he might be the father of all them that believe, though they be not circumcised, that righteousness might be imputed unto them also. Therefore, it is of faith, that it might be by grace; to the end the promise might be sure to all the seed: not to that only which is of the law, but to that also which is of the faith of Abraham, who is the father of us all." The fundamental principle underlying the church is not something detached from the Old Testament dispensation. The New and the Old stand or fall together.

In Old Testament times, the father kept his children under the influence of the worshiping community until they came to the time when they would choose for themselves. If at that time they chose to remain in the covenant with God, then they actually became covenanters themselves, individually; their relation was not changed to God. But if they should refuse to endorse the covenant which their fathers had made in their behalf, then upon their own heads came the responsibility. Could anything be more logical as a plan for Christians? Inclusion of children in the covenant community worked under what we feel was a less valuable covenant than the one we enjoy as Christians. Why should it not work under the Christian plan?

That the baptism of infants was practiced by the apostles in New Testament days seems perfectly evident.

When Peter preached at Pentecost (Acts 2:39-41) he told them that the promise was to them and to their children, and then we are told that those who received his word were baptized. It seems logical to assume that the ones were baptized who were included in the promise, and the promise included the children.

The cases of the households of Cornelius (Acts 10), of the Philippian jailor (Acts 16) and Lydia (Acts 16) are all strong in their support of the doctrine of the baptism of infants. In each of these cases the individual believed the gospel, but the household was baptized. While it is not specifically stated in any case that there were children in the families, it is logical to assume that there were. But if there were no children, then some of the adults in these families were baptized without there being any specific mention of their acceptance of the Gospel. Would it be worse to baptize children than to baptize adults who had not believed?

What of Objections?

Objection One. "There is no command to baptize infants." The best answer to this objection is that there is no command to baptize adults. The command is to preach and baptize; but neither infants nor adults are specified as the subjects.

Objection Two. "There is no command to baptize any but professing believers.

Neither is there a command to admit women to the Lord's Supper. The only right they have to the table is that which our common sense gives them, and yet no one doubts that right. It is just the same in the case of infant baptism. There is no commission to baptize infants; but there is a command to baptize the proper subjects of baptism. Since the children of believers are certainly the proper subjects, they should be baptized.

Objection Three. "Repentance (Acts 2:38) and faith (Acts 8:37) are required of those who receive baptism; therefore infants should not be baptized."

We are also taught that, except we repent, we shall perish; and, unless we believe, we shall be damned (Luke 13:3; Mark 16:16). Does this mean that infants who die in infancy will be lost? They cannot repent, and they cannot believe. The same argument which is here used against baptism would declare that they are lost. Does anyone believe that?

Objection Four. "Infants are not religious, and should not receive this sacred rite."

Are all adults who receive baptism religious? Quite often young people who are old enough to know and to make a decision for themselves are received into the church and are baptized, but they later show that the whole process meant nothing to them. Sometimes adults make a false profession and eventually are cut off from the church. In some cases these persons come back to the church and live a pious life. Do the churches require them to be baptized again? In some cases, they might request that the ceremony be repeated for their own satisfaction, but even those cases are rare.

Objection Five. "Infants do not know what it is all about, therefore it can do them no good."

The same might be said of all religious instruction given to children; they cannot appreciate it; they do not understand all that it means, and it will do them no good. Does the child appreciate the importance of learning to read and write? Does the child appreciate the importance of obeying commands?

Did the Jewish boy appreciate the rite of circumcision at the age of eight days? What good could that do in a religious way? But God established that as a ceremony to be kept.

Objection Six. "To baptize an infant chooses the form of baptism for him and destroys free agency."

The same could be said about all other teaching and training. It might be argued that the child might not want to know how to read and write when he grows up. If he should not, you would be destroying his freedom. He might not want to know about God. He might not want to obey the law. If you train him in these things before he gets old enough to appreciate them, you are destroying his freedom.

But what person believes that? To argue in that way is to say, "Throwaway all restraint. Let the children grow up to be what they want to be and to do what they want to do." If baptizing them destroys their freedom, so does all Christian teaching.

When parents brought their children to Jesus and allowed him to take them up in his arms and bless them, they were destroying the freedom of those children, according to this argument. But none of us would hesitate to do the same thing today if we had the chance.

Objection Seven. "They might be dissatisfied with their baptism later and want to be immersed."

There is no more danger of baptized children becoming dissatisfied with their baptism than with the other parts of their early training. And if it were not for the great emphasis put upon immersion by some religious sects, and the loud shouting of "much water" in their eyes, there is not the least danger of a child's ever becoming dissatisfied with his baptism.

Objection Eight. "This practice is filling the church with unconverted people."

Actual facts refute this argument. Do the churches which practice infant baptism have more unconverted people in them that those which refuse the practice? Are all the people in the churches which practice infant baptism less holy, less pure than those which refuse to practice it?

When a baptized infant reaches the time when he chooses for himself to follow Christ, then he affirms the ceremony which his parents performed for him before he was able to do it for himself. The infant baptism is not the last religious act in his life; it is one of the first of a series which culminates in his acceptance of Christ. Instead of making him less holy and less consecrated, it should make the chances for these things much greater in his life. It should be an altar upon which a fire has been burning all of the days of his life, but is finally kindled into a bright flame by his own personal decision.

What could be more inspiring to a child and youth than the knowledge that his parents had been looking forward all of his life to the time when he would accept Christ as personal Savior, and they had actually prepared the way for that acceptance? A simple personal experience of the author emphasized this fact some years ago. A mother of twin boys asked that her boys be baptized, although she had been brought up in a Baptist church. Her reason for making the request was simply that she had been keeping some little baby books for them and was planning to give them the books for their treasure when they were old enough to appreciate them. Her own statement of the case was like this: "I was always taught that it was wrong to baptize infants. But when I began to fill in the blank pages of those books and came to the page where I was to tell when and where they were baptized, I could not stand it. I knew that when those boys looked through their books they would say, 'Mother was interested in every little thing that happened to us when we were babies, but she did not care anything about our spiritual life!'" Was she right?

Another actual experience will show the force of this beautiful ceremony. A Cumberland Presbyterian elder who believed in practicing the doctrines of his church brought his little daughter to the altar to dedicate her in baptism. At the conclusion of the service an old man seventy-one years old came forward and gave his life to Christ with this testimony: "Seventy years ago my mother brought me to the altar and pledged herself to pray for my personal salvation. Up to today that prayer has been unanswered, but I want you to know that because of the memory of that scene as it was described to me and as it has been brought back to me today, her prayers of seventy years ago are now answered."

Since this is a ceremony which has behind it Divine authority, it should be highly valued. If it was wrong for the Jewish parent to neglect the ordinance which preceded this rite, it is wrong for Christian parents to neglect the ceremony which is intended to bring their children into the care of the church. The obligations which are incurred by the parents are nothing more than the obligations of all Christian parents, but they should be taken willingly by them. Every Christian has the same obligations before he joins a church that he does afterwards, but we all know that the Christian should assume the obligations of church membership.

SUBJECTS FOR FURTHER STUDY
1. Methods by which denominations which do not practice infant baptism try to take care of the needs addressed in this rite
2. The extent to which infants and minors are members of the church

10

The Lord's Supper

"The Sacrament, commonly called the Lord's Supper, was instituted by the Lord Jesus Christ at the close of His last passover supper, as a perpetual remembrance of His passion and death on the cross, by which sacrifice of Himself He was made the propitiation for the sins of the whole world" (Cumberland Presbyterian Confession of Faith, Section 104).

What Names Has This Sacrament Been Given?

The institution which we commonly call the Lord's Supper has at least four names: The Lord's Supper, the Eucharist, the Sacrament and the Communion. Each of these names refers to the same institution, but has a little different implication.

1) *"Lord's Supper"*. .. The name "The Lord's Supper" arose from the fact that it was instituted on the night in which Jesus was betrayed, as he ate his last meal with the disciples before his crucifixion. In a broad sense, the term refers to the whole supper which preceded the breaking of the bread and the drinking of the wine, and would not properly refer to the celebration we employ; but in the sense in which it is commonly employed by Protestant churches, it refers to the special part of the meal which Jesus designed as a memorial for the disciples.

2) *"Eucharist."* The "eucharist" gets its name from the fact that Jesus "gave thanks" in instituting the part of the supper we commemorate. The term "eucharist" means a thanksgiving.

3) *"Sacrament."* "Although neither this word nor the general idea appears in the New Testament, it is one of the most common terms for the Lord's Supper. The term was first used by the church historian Tertullian (end of the

second and beginning of the third century) to designate the rites of the Christian Church. "Sacrament" means an oath or covenant. With the Romans, a sacrament was an oath of fidelity to a military leader. Thus, the Lord's Supper is called a sacrament because it is a pledge, or the renewal of a pledge, of our fidelity to our Great Leader, who is the captain of our salvation. We are to fight under his banner; we are to shrink from no danger under his leadership. After such a pledge, unfaithfulness toward him would be spiritual treason.

4) *"Communion."* The term "communion" is derived from the message of Paul as found in I Corinthians 10: 16 "The cup of blessing which we bless, is it not the communion of the blood of Christ? The bread which we break, is it not the communion of the body of Christ?" It signifies a close relationship between the believer and Christ which is not one-sided, but is entered into by both parties.

What Was Its Antecedent?

The Lord's Supper is to be regarded as sustaining the same relation to the church under its present form which was sustained by the Passover to the church under its ancient form. In other words, the Passover has been superseded by the Lord's Supper. The Passover was a permanent memorial of the deliverance of the Hebrews from the bondage in Egypt. The Lord's Supper is a permanent memorial of the death of Christ, which has wrought deliverance from a bondage far more cruel and perilous than the bondage of Egypt. The Apostle seems to have some reference to this aspect of the subject when he speaks of "Christ our Passover as sacrificed for us."

"In this sacrament no sacrifice of any kind is offered for sin, but the one perfect offering of Christ as a sufficient sacrifice is set forth and commemorated by appropriate symbols. These symbols are bread and wine which, though figuratively called the body and blood of Christ, nevertheless remain, after consecration, literal bread and wine, and give no countenance to the doctrines of consubstantiation and transubstantiation" (Cumberland Presbyterian Confession of Faith, Section 105).

What Do the Symbols Used Mean?

The bread which we use in this celebration is a symbol of the body of Christ. "This is my body," said Jesus, using it as a figurative term. The bread is a symbol of the great truth that we derive our spiritual nourishment from Christ. Bread is the staff of life. Christ is the support of our spiritual life. We enjoy our natural life through him, but in a still higher sense is our spiritual life supported by him. He says of himself, "I am the living bread which came down from heaven; if any man eat of this bread, he shall live forever, and the bread that I will give is my flesh, which I will give for the life of the world" (John 6:51). Of course, the Savior speaks figuratively when he speaks thus.

The wine is the symbol of the blood of Christ. More particularly, it is a symbol of the truth that we derive our spiritual life from Christ. The shedding of his blood was his death, and through his death we live. Because he died and rose again, we live. The blood of Christ is the source of our spiritual life; the body of Christ, broken at the same time as the shedding of his blood, is represented as the supporter of this life. The blood of Christ is the price of our pardon. Condemned, we are legally dead; pardoned, we are legally alive.

There are doctrines regarding the bread and the wine which our Confession of Faith is careful to deny: the doctrines of transubstantiation and consubstantiation. They are rejected by practically all Protestant denominations. Transubstantiation is a big word which really means that the bread and wine actually become the body and blood of Jesus at the time of the ceremony. "This is my body" is taken in a literal sense.

There is no need to argue the doctrine. It seems beyond all human reason to believe that any ceremony performed by men could actually change the bread and the wine into the actual body and blood of Jesus, or that such a thing would be necessary or desirable, but this is the teaching of the Roman Catholic Church. Luther, the Father of the Reformation, rejected the doctrine of transubstantiation, but taught another which is about as bad. His doctrine, known as the doctrine of consubstantiation, is that the body and blood of Jesus are really present in the Eucharist, although the bread and wine do not actually change into them. "Christ's body is in the bread as the sword is in the scabbard, or as the Holy Ghost was in the dove, or as the fire is in a piece of hot metal." While this doctrine is above the other, it is below the simple doctrine which we accept, that the bread and wine simply *signify* the body and blood of Jesus.

The water is not changed into the Spirit at baptism, nor do we believe that the Spirit is in the water, or imparts any spiritual power to it. The water is the symbol of the Spirit. It is simply a help to us to understand the spiritual truth. So, in the Lord's Supper, *the elements are used to help us understand spiritual truths.* If we reject this simple view, we become lost in mysticism and darkness.

What Is the Sacrament?

The Sacrament is a memorial to our Savior. "This do in remembrance of me" (I Corinthians 11:24). We are forgetful. In the midst of our busy world, our minds are turned away from him who ought to be the object of thought and affection. But *when Christ is set forth crucified before our eyes in the expressive symbols of the Lord's Supper,* we *are called back from our wandering.*

It is a testimony. "For as often as ye eat this bread and drink this cup, ye do shew the Lord's death till He come" (I Corinthians 11:26). Every time we take communion, we bear testimony to the fact that Jesus died, gave his body and his blood for the sins of the world. We show that we believe that Jesus instituted this supper, that it is an historical fact to commemorate his sacrificial death.

It is a confession. "Ye do shew the Lord's death till he come." We confess that we have faith in the coming of the Lord Jesus Christ. We thus connect in our minds the suffering and the glory of Jesus-his death and his triumph.

It is a bond of union between Christians. When we commune together, we are reminded that we are members of the same body; that spiritually we have the same Christ, the same body, the same blood for I our nurture.

"As in this sacrament the communicants have visibly set before them symbols of the Savior's passion, they should not approach the holy communion without due self-examination, reverence, humility, and gratitude." "All who love the Lord Jesus in sincerity and in truth should, on all suitable occasions, express their devotion to Him by the use of the symbols of His death. But none who has not faith to discern the Lord's body should partake of His holy communion" (Cumberland Presbyterian Confession of Faith, Sections 106, 107).

The Lord's Supper is a silent sermon, telling the world that Christ died and that we are his followers. It is not a proclamation of our own goodness, of an opinion that we are better than others. In taking our place at Christ's table, we say to all men that we are sinners, that Christ died for us and that our sole dependence is upon the merits of his blood.

Some people shrink from a public confession as if it were a setting of themselves before the world as better than others-as if it were a heralding of their religion. But it is not a "profession of religion" that we make when we unite with the church and come to the Lord's Table, but a "confession of Christ." Here is a proclamation not of our own goodness, but of the death of Christ. We honor Christ, we humble ourselves; for we put ourselves behind the cross, and hide there. We are not seen at all, but it is Christ's death that is seen.

Who Should Take Communion?

The Westminster Confession states that "all ignorant and ungodly persons" should be excluded from the Communion. But we, along with the U. S. Presbyterian Church, left this statement out of our *Confession.* From this we would be justified in assuming that any person who asked to be allowed to commune in our churches, regardless of what we might think about his worthiness, should not be excluded. And, on this basis, why should anyone think that a child of believing parents be excluded who was worthy in every way to partake except for the fact that it had not yet officially joined the Church? It does not make sense to say that an adult person not a member of the Church could partake if he wanted to, but a child under the special care of the Church but not an official member, could not.

The problem complicates itself when a small child of believing parents, even previously dedicated to the Lord in baptism, but not old enough to understand the full meaning of the Communion, asks to be allowed to eat the bread and drink the wine. Admitting that it is the responsibility of the parents to instruct the child as to whether he should or should not be allowed to partake, the problem remains as to who is actually to refuse to let him take the elements if he reaches out his hand when the plate or the tray is passed. Not many elders would desire to be left with this responsibility.

It is admitted, and taught by us, that the Hebrew Passover was intended as their method of continuing religious education. It was by this means that each generation passed on to the next the principles of their faith. Little Hebrew boys who were not old enough to understand the Passover with all its significance ate it with their parents, and we can be sure that the parents took a great deal of pride in hearing a little boy, perhaps no more than three years old, ask his father, "What is the meaning of this Passover?" Modern Hebrew periodicals show pictures of little pre-school children drinking the wine which has been blessed in the Kiddush at the beginning of the Sabbath. We also teach that our Lord's Supper is a continuation of the Passover and that it is to be done "In remembrance" of Jesus. Is not this also a matter of Christian education? In what better way could a small child learn his religion than by imitating his sincere parents and then get the answers to his questions from them?

If it is not wrong for a little child to recite the Apostle's Creed merely because he is standing beside his father who is reciting it, or to sing the great hymns of the faith with his parents long before he knows what they mean and before he has made his public profession of his own faith by joining the Church, it cannot be wrong for him to eat the bread and drink the cup along with them before he is able to give a theological answer to questions regarding its meaning. There is nothing mystical about the piece of bread or the grape juice in the cup. We believe that nothing happens to them because they are used in the Communion. And it would be far wiser to risk some "desecration" of these substances than to risk the mental and spiritual problems which might arise in the mind of the pure little child who wants to worship as his parents worship but is told that he cannot do so because he is not yet a member of the Church. It would be pretty difficult to explain our practice of "open communion" to a sensible child who has been refused the elements until he has joined the Church, but who sees adults who are not members of any church admitted to the table from which he is excluded.

Our children will come much nearer to assuming all the responsibilities of the Covenant when they reach the age of accountability if we guide them from the day of their birth by precept and example in the principles and practices of the Church. We can usually do this best by following good common sense in those matters where we do not have clear scriptural bases for our actions. We can use this common sense if we always keep before us the fact that we are seeking to help people and not to perpetuate an institution.

A great many conscientious persons have held back from the communion because of their interpretation of First Corinthians 11:27. They feel that the verse refers to them. But it is the *manner* of receiving the sacrament that is referred to. In a certain sense, no one is worthy, for all are sinners. But the gospel is for sinners who will confess their sins and believe on Christ as a personal Savior. All who sincerely trust Christ and are striving to follow him are welcome at the table of our Lord, regardless of what denominational connection they may have, or whether they have any. The only requirement is that they see in the symbols the representation of the broken body and shed blood of Jesus Christ and be reminded of his sacrifice for them, their own hearts being the judge.

SUGGESTIONS FOR FURTHER STUDY
1. The origin, meaning and celebration of the Passover (Exodus 12:3ff.)
2. The account of the institution of the Lord's Supper in the New Testament, with the manner of observing the Supper (John 13)
3. The meaning of "due self-examination, reverence, humility, and gratitude"
4. The teachings of the church fathers on the Lord's Supper
5. The proper manner of administering the Lord's Supper in the Churches. Sections 18-20, Directory of Worship
6. The evil practices growing up around the Lord's Supper in the early Church, as revealed in Paul's letters
7. The values derived from the proper observance of the Lord's Supper

11

Things to Come

"The bodies of men, after death, return to dust; but their spirits, being immortal, return to God who gave them. The spirits of the righteous are received into heaven, where they behold the face of God in light and glory, waiting for the full redemption of their bodies; and the spirits of the wicked are cast into hell, where they are reserved to the judgment of the great day. The Scriptures speak of no other place for departed spirits.

"At the resurrection, those who are alive shall not die, but be changed; and all the dead shall be raised up, spiritual and immortal, and spirits and bodies be reunited forever. There shall be a resurrection both of the just and the unjust; of the unjust to dishonor, and of the just unto honor; the bodies of the latter shall be fashioned like *unto* Christ's glorious body.

"God has appointed a day wherein He will judge the world in righteousness by Jesus Christ-to whom all power and judgment are given by the Father-in which not only the apostate angels shall be judged, but likewise all persons who have lived upon earth shall appear before the tribunal of Christ, and shall receive according to what they have done, whether good or evil.

"After the judgment, the wicked shall go away into eternal punishment, but the righteous unto eternal life" (Cumberland Presbyterian Confession of Faith, Sections 112-115).

What Is the Place of Abode of Departed Spirits?

Thus closes our Confession of Faith, and in these brief sentences we have all that our church has to say about things to come. Notice that one distinguishing characteristic is brought out in the first paragraph: "The Scriptures speak of no other place for departed spirits." This is a distinguishing

91

doctrine of our church, along with other Protestant groups. The Roman Catholic Church teaches that there is another place for departed spirits, called Purgatory. Their doctrine is, "Purgatory is a place where souls are detained for a time and purified if they die guilty of slight sins, or if they have not entirely atoned for grave sins, though these have been forgiven." "We can help souls in Purgatory by our prayers, by Indulgences and especially by the Sacrifice of the Mass." Our Confession of Faith clearly indicates that we do not believe this. We believe that our souls go to heaven or to hell according to whether or not we have been saved by Christ.

What of the Resurrection of the Body?

The doctrine of the resurrection of the body is wholly a doctrine of revelation. There are many analogies in the natural world, but they are merely illustrations and prove nothing. The revival of things at the coming of spring is one of the most common and most beautiful illustrations. It is often referred to at the Easter season. The things seem to be dead and then burst forth into life. But the illustration fails at the most important point: the things were not actually dead. For that reason, the illustration is just a reminder and nothing more. All we really know about the doctrine is that which the Bible teaches.

Some people deny that the Old Testament had anything to say about the resurrection. While it is true that the Old Testament is not as clear on the subject as is the New Testament, we must admit that many Jews believed in the resurrection, and it is impossible to account for their belief except that they got it from their scriptures. The two main parties among them at the time of the coming of Jesus were the Pharisees and the Sadducees. One of their chief points of difference was on the subject of the resurrection. The Pharisees believed in the resurrection and the Sadducees did not. It is difficult to understand where they got their doctrine if the Old Testament does not teach something about it.

The writer of Hebrews (11:17-19) taught that Abraham believed in the resurrection. He said that Abraham offered up Isaac in the belief "that God was able to raise him from the dead, from whence also he received him in a figure."

Daniel 12:2 says, "Many of them that sleep in the dust of the earth shall awake, some to everlasting life, and some to shame and everlasting contempt."

In the prophecy of Isaiah (26:19) we have an expression which, regardless of what it teaches directly, has beneath it belief in the resurrection. "Thy dead men shall live; together with my dead body shall they arise."

The most popular of the Old Testament passages is the triumphant expression of Job (19:25-27). "For I know my redeemer liveth, and that he shall stand at the latter day upon the earth; and though after my skin worms destroy this body, yet in my flesh shall I see God." The testimony of these men is sufficient to prove that a number of thinking Jews did have a belief in immortality. Perhaps if we had more of the writings of their times instead of just the small portion which has been preserved for us, we would find that many of them did express their views and that their views were similar to ours on this important subject.

Jesus taught that there would be a resurrection and a judgment. John 5:28, 29, and Luke 14:14 are definite teachings of his on this subject. Paul also made much of the doctrine of the resurrection. Whenever he wished to make his defense and release certain, he would refer to the resurrection, and immediately the Jews would become entangled in an argument and some would side with Paul against the others. One of the charges brought against him at one of his trials was that he taught the resurrection of the dead. In writing to the Corinthians he gave us one of our most beautiful chapters on this subject, chapter 15 of First Corinthians. Also in First Thessalonians 3:14 Paul links the resurrection of the dead with the fact of the resurrection of Christ, upon which our belief in the doctrine really rests.

As we think about so great and so mysterious questions, there are many problems that cannot be understood by our finite minds. Reason cannot answer them, for human reasoning is limited by things that are finite. The resurrection deals with spiritual, infinite things. Our only source of wisdom on this subject is derived from the Word of God.

What of the Judgment?

The same can be said about the question of the Judgment. The judgment is a sequel to the resurrection. Our Confession of Faith does not attempt to draw a blueprint of all that will take place, but it does assert that there will be a judgment of all who have ever lived on the earth and Christ will be the Judge. Although we may not be able to understand just when it will take place and how all of the things will be carried on, we may rest assured that every thought, every word, every action will be properly judged, for Christ will be the unerring Judge. With Christ as the Judge, much of the natural dread of the day is taken away. The same justice, impartiality, and truth will be exercised in that day as were exercised in the life of Jesus while he was on earth. To those who believe in Christ, this is enough to know.

What of the Second Coming?

The Second Coming of Christ is a doctrine of the Scriptures, and the Cumberland Presbyterian Church therefore believes in it; but there is no formal statement in the Confession of Faith which sets forth the particular interpretation of this doctrine which we accept. Probably it is safe to say that practically all of the major interpretations could find support among some of our people. The silence of the Confession of Faith on the subject is doubtless due to the fact that this matter was not seriously at issue at the time of the adoption of our statement of doctrine. The closing statement of the Presbyterian Confession upon which ours was based is "Come, Lord Jesus, come quickly." This is the final statement of a discussion of the purpose of the Judgment. But when our church fathers decided upon our statement, they did not leave even this much reference to the coming of Jesus in their Confession. Whether this change was deliberate or because of a lack of concern about the doctrine, we cannot tell at this distance. All we know is that they did not make a statement about it.

What of the Millennium?

The same is true of the question of the millennium, or the thousand years about which there is so much dispute. Our church fathers did not see fit to make any statement about this matter. During recent years there have been attempts to get the denomination to adopt a certain position on it, but all of these attempts have been refused. The statement of the 1941 General Assembly, a sufficient answer to these requests, is as follows:

> We have had under consideration the memorial from McAdow Presbytery regarding the Cumberland Presbyterian Church's position on the millennium referred to us by this body. After some discussion and prayerful consideration of this memorial, your committee recommends that it be not granted. We would urge, however, that we as members of the body of Christ be charitable and patient with each other as to our interpretation of the Scripture. God's Word tells us that it is not in the province of man to legislate on such mysteries (John 16:13). We feel that it is significant that for 131 years the fathers of our Church have not deemed it wise to speak dogmatically on this subject, doubtless realizing the danger of disputes, controversies, and divisions which might be involved therein (Page 147 of the 1941 Assembly Minutes).

Since that time there have been other attempts to say just what the denomination believes on this question, but the discussion has often provoked more heat than light, and has always been put aside for that reason. As a consequence of this division of opinion and the controversy which the question invariably provokes, the denomination remains without a definite position, and each individual is left to choose for himself what seems to be the most plausible theory. Any position you choose can be supported by some passages of scripture, but none of them will be the position of the Cumberland Presbyterian Church, for it has no position on these subjects.

There are a few facts regarding the Second Coming of Christ which may be of interest and value.

What Are the Facts Regarding the Second Coming?

1) The New Testament teaches that the Second Coming is to be an outward, visible, and personal return of Christ. This seems to be clear from the teachings of Jesus and the later writings of the New Testament. Read Acts 1:11; First Thessalonians 4:16; Second Peter 3:3-12; James 5:8; and Revelation 22: 12.

2) The exact time of the personal return of Christ is unrevealed. Jesus said that he himself did not know the day and the hour. Read Matthew 24:36; Mark 13:32; and Acts 1:7. In the writings of Paul and the words of Jesus, there seems to be much more concern over the devotion of the people to their tasks and practical duties than over the knowledge of details regarding the future.

3) Jesus seems to have recognized subordinate comings in addition to the Second Coming in this visible and personal aspect. He promised that he would come and make his abode in the disciples in the form of the Holy Spirit. It is this fact which is confusing to many. Some think that this is what Jesus was attempting to teach along with the idea of the ultimate triumph of the Kingdom. These people would reject the idea of the physical and personal return of Christ.

4) The general attitude of the New Testament writers toward the Second Coming was one of constant expectancy. To all of them the Coming was always imminent. There is no doubt that Paul and his followers expected to see it in their lifetime. That was one of the great problems with the Thessalonians who quit work just to wait for it, and the other members who wondered if their loved ones who had died before the return of Jesus would have a share in this Second Coming or if they had lost its benefits by their untimely death.

5) This constant expectancy served two good purposes in the Church. First, it was a source of great consolation and devotion. These people lived in a time of great trial and suffering. The thought of the return of their Lord furnished the kind of help they needed to help them to endure. Second, this belief gave unity to the church. They were all followers of the Christ who had come and would come again. He was always keeping watch above his own and was waiting until the time when they would all be gathered to him.

On the question of the Millennium there is far less agreement than on the question of the Second Coming of Christ. The Millennium is the period of the thousand years' reign of the saints with Christ on the earth. The passage in which reference is made to it is Revelation 20:1-6. There are many degrees of belief within the two leading schools on the question, the pre-millennialists and the post-millennialists, but their chief difference is on whether or not the Coming of Christ will precede or follow the thousand years. Pre-millennialists hold that the coming of Christ will precede the period of the thousand years.

Here is a general outline of their view: 1) When Christ returns the world will be under the power of evil. 2) At his Coming Christ will win a great victory over His enemies and will destroy the Antichrist. 3) Living Christians will be caught up to meet the Lord in the air. 4) The first resurrection of the dead in Christ will take place at the beginning of the millennium. 5) Then follows a judgment of the living nations and the saints will reign with Christ for a thousand years. 6) At the end of this thousand years there will be a return of great wickedness because Satan, who has been bound, will now be loosed. 7) Then there will be the resurrection of the wicked, the final judgment, and the eternal awards. There are many other minor items included in this belief by different ones of its advocates, and there are many passages of scripture which are used to support the belief.

Post-millennialists hold that the millennial period will be the result of the gradual spread of the gospel and its conquest over all departments of human life. At the end of this period the conflict between good and evil will be resumed, after which Christ will return in person. Then will take place the resurrection of the righteous and the wicked, the final judgment, and the eternal awards.

Another group would assert that all of these questions of the Second Coming and the Millennium have been misunderstood and exaggerated by a literal interpretation of the Scriptures. They would insist that these ideas were advanced to teach spiritual truths and are not intended to be interpreted literally.

None of these beliefs is the doctrine of the Cumberland Presbyterian Church, for it has no doctrine on this question. The only accepted doctrine we have on the millennium is that "we as members of the body of Christ be charitable and patient with each other as to our interpretation of the Scriptures;" that it is not in the province of man to legislate on such mysteries.

GENERAL BOOKS ON THEOLOGY

Beard, Richard: *Lectures on Theology,* 3 volumes, Board of Publication of the Cumberland Presbyterian Church, 1870. (Out of print.)

Blake, T. C.: *Theology Condensed.* Cumberland Presbyterian Publishing House, 1883.

Crisman, E. B.: *Origin and Doctrines of the Cumberland Presbyterian Church,* 1877.

Strong, A. H.: *Outlines of Systematic Theology.* Judson Press, 1908.

Clarke, W. N.: *An Outline of Christian Theology,* Scribner's, 1899.

Hodge, A. A.: *Outlines of Theology,* Eerdamans, 1928.

Mullins, E. Y.: The Christian Religion in Its Doctrinal Expression, Judson Press, 1917.

Foster, R. V.: *Systematic Theology,* Cumberland Presbyterian Publishing House, 1898.

Davidson, A. B.: *The Theology of the Old Testament,* Scribner's, 1917.

Stevens, G. B.: *The Theology of the New Testament,* Scribner's, 1914. Fisher, G. P.: *History of Christian Doctrine,* Scribner's, 1919.